The 7 SPIRITUAL PRACTICES of MARRIAGE

The 7 Spiritual Practices *of* MARRIAGE

Your Guide to Creating a Deep and Lasting Love

Kevin Anderson, Ph.D.

CLB PRESS

Anderson, Kevin E., 1960—
    The Seven Spiritual Practices of Marriage: Your Guide to Creating a Deep and Lasting Love/
    Kevin E. Anderson
    ISBN: 0972835505

PRINTED IN THE UNITED STATES OF AMERICA

TO THE COUPLE:
WHAT YOU'LL LEARN BY READING THIS BOOK

This book presents an intentional model of marriage. Intentional means that a great marriage is created *on purpose*. *The Seven Spiritual Practices of Marriage* will show you how you can, day by day, through your commitment to seven key practices, experience the full potential of married life. Each of these practices is a way of living out a core spiritual truth upon which it rests. Together these seven practices will allow your marriage to become a committed, intimate, passionate, and spiritual journey. You'll discover that marriage, though not always an easy or predictable venture, is far richer, deeper, and more wonderful than you imagined it could be. You'll also see that marriage is about much more than simply trying to "stay in love."

In this book you'll learn how to:

◆ Create an ongoing marital visioning process that will keep you moving toward your personal and marital goals and dreams.

◆ Remain affectionately and emotionally connected with each other on a daily basis.

◆ Resolve conflicts in ways that honor you both and turn discord into a path to deeper intimacy.

◆ Give up the search for the perfect lover by accepting and affirming the person you have chosen to love for life.

◆ Work on individual "habit energies" that may be holding you and your marriage back.

◆ Keep your marriage passionate by maintaining an other-centered, gifting approach to sexual loving.

◆ Become spiritual companions as you walk the sacred path through life together.If you're willing to invest time and energy into the seven practices and to continue learning about them throughout your years together, your marriage will become a deep, lasting, and extraordinary love!

LANGUAGE, INTENDED AUDIENCE, AND LIMITATIONS

The Seven Spiritual Practices of Marriage is intended for both married and engaged couples. Throughout the book, I have used the words "spouse," "partner," "husband," and "wife" in reference to the individuals who make up a couple. It would simply have been too awkward to write "spouse/fiancé/fiancee" or other attempts at inclusiveness throughout. Furthermore, the book introduces an intentional and spiritual model of married life. Engaged couples should have little difficulty reading the book as a guide to married life as they hope to experience it soon.

Although some sections of *The Seven Spiritual Practices of Marriage* discuss family life, this is not a book about parenting. The emphasis here is on the relationship between the woman and man who have chosen to marry. An adequate treatment of all that is involved in creating a beautiful family would require its own volume. Couples with children will find that most of the principles in this book can be extended into their efforts to create an extraordinary family.

Finally, this book is for couples who want to make their marriages as good as they can be. It contains many ideas that can benefit your marriage. *The Seven Spiritual Practices of Marriage* **is not, however, intended to function as a substitute for professional counseling in situations that require more than can be addressed by a book. If your marriage is less than you would like it to be or is seriously struggling, please consider the help of a competent marriage counselor.**

If you find this book helpful, please share it with others. By passing on what you learn here, you will become part of the important work of helping couples intentionally create loving and lasting marriages based on deep and daily honoring. It's difficult to imagine what this world needs more.

Kevin Anderson
Monclova, Ohio

January, 2005

TABLE OF CONTENTS

Foreword 11

Introduction: You Can Create a Truly Extraordinary Marriage! 15

Practice #1: Create a Shared Vision 27

    Decide to build a Namaste marriage 31

    Hold regular visioning meetings. 32

    Guidelines for positive visioning meetings 34

    What to do in your first visioning meeting. 35

    Following through with action 37

    How to keep visioning meetings interesting 38

    Be a boulder in the torrent of the culture 40

    Keep first things first 43

    Nurture three sets of dreams 45

    Keep it clean 46

Practice #2: Make Connection the Norm. 53

    Share each other's life interests 57

    Make sure your spouse is dated 58

    Create a culture of affection 59

    Do an OIL check regularly 61

    Speak your spouse's love language 62

    Stay heart to heart 64

    The high/low question 64

    Love letters for 20/20 marital vision. 65

Practice #3: Bring Honoring to Conflict 73

    The seven-step model of conflict resolution. 77

    The seven-step model: Susan and Mark. 78

    Step 1: Have the conflict. 80

    Step 2: Use time-outs to stop destructive interactions 81

    Step 3: Reconnect after conflict. 83

    Step 4: Exchange mutual, no-fault apologies. 85

Step 5: Use empathic listening to review the conflict 87
    Staying in role. 88
    Using "I language" 89
    Guidelines for empathic listening 90
    Using reflections 92
    Reflecting feelings and "Tell me more" 92
Nonverbal communication 94
Step 6: Solve solvable problems. 96
Step 7: Enjoy feeling connected again 97
Bring honoring to recurrent conflicts 98
Look for the dream behind the conflict 101

Practice #4: Give Up the Search for the Perfect Lover **107**
Know your template for the perfect lover. 111
Accept your partner's preference for :
    Introversion or Extroversion 113
    Sensible Realism or Intuitive Idealism. 116
    Thinking or Feeling 118
    Judicious Organization or Predictable Spontaneity 119
Don' just habituate—celebrate! 121
Accept longing as a part of being human 122

Practice #5: Work on the "I" in Marriage. **127**
A closer look at habit energies 131
The four harbingers of happiness 133
Male and female roles habit energies 134
Health habit energies 136
Thinking habit energies 137
Emotional habit energies 139
Affection habit energies 140
Conflict habit energies. 141
Sexual habit energies 142
Work habit energies. 144
Money habit energies 145
Parenting habit energies 146
Spiritual habit energies. 146
Mutual mentoring 148

Practice #6: Make Love a Gift **153**

The gift exchange model 155
The gift of reciprocal energies. 159
The gift of creating a shared sexual vision. 161
The gift of enjoying four kinds of touch. 163
Six principles for creating a shared sexual vision. 164
The gift of communicating about sexual problems 167
Common sexual problems in marriage. 169
The gift of communicating about sexual rhythms. 170

Practice #7: Walk the Sacred Path. **177**

Seeing Divinity in disguise 183
Remember that joy means God is present. 184
Unmask God in hard times 185
Giving voice to God awareness 186
Consider "I love you" a prayer and say it often. 187
Offer Meister Eckhart's prayer daily 188
Ask, "Where did you encounter God today?" 189
Ritualizing God awareness 190
Share meals as a sacred rite of the home 190
Frame the day in a sacred way 192
Create a shared vision for involvement in a spiritual community 193
Serving from God awareness. 194
Build your marriage at the crossroads. 195
Help heal the world as you heal yourselves. 197
See creating a Namaste marriage as a gift to the world 199

Namaste definition and acronym for remembering the seven practices. 202
Epilogue: Seven Practices, One Extraordinary Marriage 203
　　　　　　Diamond in the Middle. 205
Appendix A Going Beyond Ordinary: A Sampling of Marriage Research 206
Appendix B Keep It Clean: Prevent Toxins from Poisoning Your Marriage 208
Appendix C Empathic Listening:
　　　　　　An Extended Example and Further Considerations. 217
Appendix D Resistance to Creating an Extraordinary Marriage. 220

Acknowlegdments, About the Cover Art, Permissions 223

This book is dedicated to

ROBERT AND MARY JO ANDERSON
(MARRIED 1954-2002)

who taught me that a great marriage takes practice.

Foreword

It is not recorded in the book of Genesis, but I suspect that as Adam and Eve were being expelled from the Garden of Eden, the first wife turned to the first husband and said, "You know, honey, it's tough living in an age of transition!" It seems to me that every age is an age of transition, and a married couple faces many changes in their life together, no matter who they are and when they live. The pace of change in our time is dramatic—more relentless, I believe, than at any other time in history. So much change puts great pressure on the institution of marriage and on married couples.

As a priest and counselor for nearly forty years who has prepared over five hundred couples for marriage, I have seen some significant changes in the social forces that affect marriage:

- Couples today do not presume the clearly-defined roles of earlier generations.
- The increase in life expectancy makes "until death do us part" a much longer commitment and requires a couple to learn to keep growing together through the stages of adult life.
- Greater mobility in our society, which results in couples moving away from their families of origin and childhood friends, necessitates the establishment of new support systems.
- The revolution in sexual mores and a casual attitude toward sex in our culture makes fidelity more difficult to maintain and beautiful sex in marriage less likely.
- Our "culture of divorce" no longer encourages couples to stay together through good times and bad.
- The increase in interfaith unions, now at about 45% of all marriages, leaves many couples struggling to develop a shared bond of faith and spiritual intimacy.

Marriage has existed throughout human history, but experts say that we have only recently entered an age in which people freely choose their marriage partners based on a mutual exchange of love. This experience of freedom offers the possibility for a satisfying marriage, but the high expectation for love, combined with a limited understanding of what love is in the long run of married life, carry the potential for disillusionment and the shattering of couples' dreams.

When two people fall in love and decide to marry, they embark upon one of the most rewarding relationships ever created by God, but also one of the most challenging. Many couples believe that the powerful feelings that motivate their decision to marry are enough to create a healthy marriage. Very quickly, however, couples discover that their feelings of love fluctuate. They sense that the love they felt at the beginning of their relationship is not enough to sustain an intimate marriage, but many couples experience this primarily as a loss rather than an invitation to a deeper and more mature love.

In *The Seven Spiritual Practices of Marriage*, Dr. Kevin Anderson has given couples a much-needed model for building a great marriage on purpose. His emphasis on the intentional use of the seven practices is just what couples need to avoid becoming another divorce statistic. Dr. Anderson has given couples a profoundly hopeful and practical guide to the best that married life has to offer. By meeting regularly to discuss their marital vision, keeping connected day-by-day, handling conflict with honoring, giving up the search for the perfect lover by offering unconditional acceptance, working on individual habit energies, enjoying the gift of sexuality, and seeing Divinity in the disguise of daily married life, couples can create deeply loving and enduring marriages. Dr. Anderson's vision of married love goes way beyond "how to keep that lovin' feeling." It gives couples a set of practices for creating a loving marriage day by day.

Grounded in his own loving relationships with Claudia and their five children, and influenced by the beautiful forty-eight-year marriage of his parents, Kevin Anderson is a truly insightful and gifted writer, psychologist, father and husband. This book is one to be read and reread. My hope is that your copy becomes worn and dog-eared from repeated consultation throughout many years of living extraordinarily ever after.

Rev. Daniel J. Zak
Pastor, St. Richard Catholic Church
Swanton, Ohio

January, 2005

The 7 Spiritual Practices *of* Marriage

The Seven Spiritual Practices of Marriage

INTRODUCTION:

YOU CAN CREATE A
TRULY EXTRAORDINARY MARRIAGE!

"What is THAT?!" our fourteen-year-old daughter exclaimed. "That's the most ridiculous thing I've ever seen!" she added with typical teen hyperbole. Then she fell on the floor laughing.

She was looking at a picture of me and Claudia, my wife of twenty years, in the local paper. There we were, caught by the photographer in the Namaste* greeting—hands in the prayer position in front of the heart, heads tilted forward in a bow to one another. The photo appeared with a feature article about a workshop I was offering on the the seven spiritual practices of marriage.

"We bow that way to each other every morning," I told our daughter. "It means today will be a day of honoring in our marriage."

"Well I still think it's ridiculous," she replied.

"Namaste" (the word together with the bow) is a greeting used in some parts of Asia. I've seen various translations of it. In casual use it simply means hello or goodbye. In a more spiritual sense it means, "my spirit greets your spirit" or, "God in me greets God in you."

In less than five seconds every morning, Claudia and I reaffirm our commitment to keep our marriage based on a deeply honoring way of thinking about the relationship that translates into our best efforts to treat each other in a loving way every day. The energy this simple greeting creates recalls Victor Hugo's wonderful line: "To love another person is to see the face of God."

Although love is a powerful impetus for husbands and wives to help and support each other, to make each other happy, and to create a family, it does not in itself create the substance of the relationship—personal qualities and skills that are crucial to sustain and make it grow.

AARON BECK

* Namaste ("nah-mah-stay")—see page 202 for how this word can be used as an acronym to remember the seven practices.

15

When a marriage fails, the amount of *dishonoring* that has come to be the norm is sad. Dishonoring can take many forms: sarcasm, open fighting, giving the silent treatment or cold shouldering, lack of priority spending quality time together, workaholism, defensiveness, criticism, abusive language, withdrawal of sexual attention—to name just a few. In some struggling marriages the dishonoring is not dramatic—but there is no consistent effort to create daily honoring interactions. This can allow a marriage to drift toward divorce.

Over time, marriages that fail have one thing in common: The couple does not maintain a daily commitment to treat one another in a kind, loving, honoring way. Without such a commitment, the once juicy grape of young love can shrivel into the raisin of disappointment, resentment, or resignation.

The Seven Spiritual Practices of Marriage is about how to create a Namaste marriage on purpose. If creating a marriage that is spiritual at its core sounds boring comparred to the promises of great sex on the covers of magazines in the grocery store checkout line, it's not. Making honoring the daily norm of your relationship will help you create the best possible version of your marriage, including the sexual part.

Throughout this book I refer to a marriage based on deep and daily honoring alternatively as a Namaste marriage or an extraordinary marriage. By "extraordinary" I mean a marriage that goes *beyond* the ordinary; that is, the couple invests far more time and energy than is typical into creating a shared vision for the marriage and into intentionally making their vision a reality. An extraordinary marriage also goes *beneath* the ordinary. The partners in such a marriage are tuned into and regularly call attention to the sacredness that is just below the surface of their ordinary lives.

A SPIRITUAL MODEL OF DAILY MARRIED LIFE

To love another person is to see the face of God.

VICTOR HUGO

Most marriages proceed from day to day, week to week, and year to year without a clear guiding vision. Couples are often in agreement about certain material goals, such as building a new house together, but lack a shared vision for the kind of *relationship* they want to build together. This is because couples rarely talk directly about the question, "What kind of marriage do we want to create from this day forward?" In Namaste marriages, this question is revisited repeatedly throughout the couple's life together.

In addition to lacking a guiding vision, ordinary marriages are not as happy as they could be—or end in divorce—because the couple simply has no clear idea of *how* to build a better relationship. Too many married people embark on goals—building homes, starting new jobs, having a baby—hoping for renewed life in the marriage, only to find that old, problematic relationship patterns persist.

This book presents a model of marriage based on a spiritual view of married life. All of the ideas in this book rest on the concept that marriage is a graced and sacred way to live. In creating an extraordinary, Namaste marriage, spouses travel a spiritual path of continuous growth and discovery that winds through each day of their life together.

In calling marriage spiritual or sacred, I'm referring mainly to the potential of daily married life (sharing meals, doing chores, working through conflicts, taking trips, making love, raising children) to reveal the surprising presence of God beneath the routine. It is the awareness that there is a deeper layer to daily existence that gives married love such a vast potential.

Ordinary marriages are not based on a spiritual model. They flow, rather, with the secular model of marriage in the culture. I call this the *default model.* If you don't deliberately base your marriage on something more solid, you will default to the secular model, which is woefully insufficient for even staying married, not to mention experiencing the best of marriage. The secular model results in a lack of clarity about priorities, too much busyness, a primary focus on material goals, an experience of sex that is less than it can be, and a lack of heart-to-heart and spiritual connection. In other words, the default model can lead to a generally stressed-out, hectic, disconnected, less-than-satisfy-

It doesn't happen all at once. You become. It takes a long time.

Margery Williams

ing experience of married life. Many people assume this is just the way married life is—that the ordinary, default model of marriage is as good as it gets. It's not, as you'll discover in the pages ahead.

WHAT A NAMASTE MARRIAGE IS *NOT*

It's important to clear up four misconceptions about the idea of Namaste marriage. First, this model is not just about being happy. Living extraordinarily ever after is different from and actually more attainable than living "happily ever after." Happiness is a by-product in both life and marriage. We generally experience more of it when we cultivate health in body, mind, and spirit. We cannot, however, force it to be ours in every moment or season of life. By saying we are working toward an extraordinary marriage, then, we need not come across as holier-than-thou or happier-than-thou. A marriage is made extraordinary by dedication to a process of continuing to learn and grow, not by whatever level of happiness has been attained.

Second, Namaste marriages are far from flawless. Perfect marriages do not exist. People in these extraordinary marriages have conflicts, experience boredom, get out of sync sexually, and miscommunicate about routine and important matters. What makes a marriage extraordinary is not that it is always smooth sailing. In these marriages, couples eventually realize that hard times hold lessons that cannot be taught by good times. In such marriages, all the experiences of the marriage (with the exception of the toxic behaviors in Appendix B) are accepted as potential contributors to personal and spiritual growth.

Third, a Namaste marriage is not something you can have and hold onto any more than you could have a great golf game and expect it to stay in top form without continuing to play frequently. I'm always impressed when the best golfers in the world go back to their coaches to get input on what's not quite right with their swings. These players are at the top of their sport in part because they have the attitude of professionals, which includes a commitment to ongoing learning and fine-tuning.

Most marriages slip back much more quickly than a golf swing when the partners stop putting in the intentional energy necessary to keep on course.

Finally, a Namaste marriage is not an island or an end unto itself. Creating a wonderful marriage that remains confined to our own private world is not what this book is about. An Namaste marriage has a spiritual core, which implies that the couple strives to find ways to be of service to the world.

AN OVERVIEW OF THE SEVEN PRACTICES

The diagram below depicts how the seven practices interlock and together form the bigger picture—a Namaste marriage.

This book's title refers to the *seven spiritual practices*, but throughout the book I refer to them more often as just the *seven practices*. It is important to keep in mind, however, that I consider them *spiritual* practices because each one is based on a core spiritual truth to which we return again and again throughout married life. These truths are conveyed by the spiritual focus passage on the first page of each chapter. For us mortals (yes, that includes both of you!), these seven spiritual truths are sufficiently challenging that we never really get them figured out, nailed down, or mastered once and for all.

The emphasis on seven spiritual *practices*, then, is important because it reminds us that these practices only help us discover the great potential of committed love as long as we continue practicing them throughout our married lives. Each practice represents a spiritual principle that we attempt to translate into specific, repeatable behaviors that create a deep and lasting love. These practices must be put into practice regularly, in some cases daily, in order for the great potential of marriage to be revealed.

The table on page 21 summarizes the seven practices and how working with them can transform the experience of marriage from ordinary to extraordinary. In each case, the practice shifts us from a nonconscious belief about marriage to a conscious choice. The shift is from passive acceptance of the secular, default model to the active practice of a model designed to intentionally makes marriage richer and rewarding.

Living your marriage from conscious, intentional energy will produce far better fruit than living it from unconscious, default energy.

Every chapter of this book is about becoming more conscious and intentional about marriage. Chapter 1 gets us started with *Create a shared vision*. This central key is about meeting with one another regularly to continue dreaming about the life you want to build together—and taking action steps toward your goals.

In chapter 2 you'll learn about *Make connection the norm*—the important practice of ensuring that connecting, loving behaviors occur daily in your marriage. When connection is the norm,

PRACTICE	NONCONSCIOUS BELIEFS: ORDINARY MARRIAGE	CONSCIOUS CHOICES: EXTRAORDINARY MARRIAGE
CREATE A SHARED VISION	Good marriages are made in heaven.	Good marriages are the result of a shared vision and daily actions that make that vision reality.
MAKE CONNECTION THE NORM	Loving feelings lead to loving behaviors.	Loving words and behaviors create loving feelings and relationships.
BRING HONORING TO CONFLICT	Good marriages should have no conflict; OR Conflict is loud, hurtful, and scary.	Good marriages approach conflict with mutually honoring energy and make it a pathway to deeper intimacy.
GIVE UP THE SEARCH FOR THE PERFECT LOVER	For every person there is a perfect soulmate.	Marriage at its best is about accepting each other as human, finite soul companions. Only God is the Perfect Lover.
WORK ON THE "I" IN MARRIAGE	"Our marriage would be fine if my partner would change."	A good marriage blossoms from the continuing efforts of both individuals to grow personally and spiritually.
MAKE LOVE A GIFT	Sex in marriage is about getting your needs met OR Sex isn't important—it's just for procreation.	Sex in marriage is a sacred way of creating new life and of gifting your partner with love and pleasure.
WALK THE SACRED PATH	The routines of daily life are hazardous to deep and enduring love.	Daily married life is sacred. It gives frequent opportunities to experience God's extraordinary presence in the ordinary.

conflict is experienced as an unwelcome interruption, and the couple is motivated to address the conflict and return to connection.

Bring honoring to conflict (chapter 3) presents a model for approaching conflict in a way that can deepen your intimacy rather than create more discord or distance between you. You'll learn about time-outs, reconnecting, no-fault apologies, and an almost magically effective approach to listening deeply to your partner.

Chapter 4 will help you to *Give up the search for the perfect lover.* This key practice focuses on the importance of accepting one's partner *as is*—and the paradoxical truth that people often grow in surprising ways when they are genuinely accepted. This practice is about not making your spouse into a home improvement project—and about realizing that only God is the Perfect Lover.

In Chapter 5, you'll learn about how to *Work on the "I" in marriage.* The greatest leverage for creating a better marriage is not in trying to change your partner, but in improving your own ability to be a genuinely loving person and spouse.

Chapter 6 is the one about sex (go ahead, turn right to it if you must!). *Make love a gift* is the practice of married sexuality in an other-centered, life-giving, exciting, pleasurable, and sacred way. Even marriage veterans, or perhaps especially marriage veterans, will learn a thing or two here about keeping passion alive and well in marriage.

In chapter 7, Walk the sacred path, you'll read about various ways to make your daily experience of marriage a deep, purposeful, spiritual walk through life. This final practice may not sound as interesting as the sex chapter, but it is really the special ingredient that makes the whole recipe.

How to Use This Book

Though they are presented one chapter after another, the seven practices really form an integrated whole. To be most effective, each one depends on our working with the other six. *Bring hon-*

oring to conflict (practice #3), for instance, isn't really possible if we don't *Make connection the norm* on a daily basis (practice #2). Likewise, *Make love a gift* (practice #6) clearly requires the active awareness and use of of the other six practices. I recommend that you first read all the way through the book and orient yourself to the whole model of Namaste marriage, instead of focusing quickly on one or two practices. Some readers may find it helpful to take a quick tour through the book first, reading the summaries at the beginning and end of each chapter to get an overview of the seven-practice model. Going back for a more careful reading will fill out your knowledge of what's involved in putting these practices into action in your marriage. You may also find the self-assessment tool on page 25 helpful for clarifying which practices are most important for you to focus on first.

When you begin attempting an active application of the seven practices, you will find that the practices of *Make connection the norm* and *Bring honoring to conflict* are particularly important to opening up your experience of the other five practices. Good things happen when you fill your daily life with kindness, affection, and a deep honoring of one another. While *Create a shared vision* is central to the model, effective visioning is not possible without good connection and the ability to handle conflict in an honoring way.

Most of the main concepts in this book are followed by a Key Suggestion exercise to help you get started discussing and using these practices. These and are contained in shaded boxes and are designated by a key symbol (⚷). Don't give up if some of these exercises create tension. This book is not seven simple steps to a great marriage. If tension comes up as you begin to embrace this model, consider it a normal part of learning to live marriage at a higher level, and be sure to study practice #3 (*Bring honoring to conflict*) carefully. Remember, you don't need to do every single idea in this book. Pick the lowest-hanging fruit first; that is, try the ideas that seem to fit your relationship well and appear to be readily achievable. Later you can try ideas that at first seemed like too much of a stretch.

The quotations included in the margins throughout the book may serve as good discussion starters as you work your way through it. There are many colloquial expressions in the culture that do not support a spiritual view of marriage (for example, "Why ruin a good friendship by marrying?"). Perhaps the worst example of the kind of misguided ideas that married people pick up was relayed to me by a client. "My friend told me that if a marriage is work, that's a sign that it's wrong for you." Married couples need wisdom that can inspire them on the journey. I hope some of the dozens of quotations included in these pages will do that for you.

Every chapter contains four additional features. First, as an invitation to pause and reflect, a "nested meditation" on each of the seven practices is included near the beginning of each chapter (see sample, page 30). These meditations are from my book *Divinity in Disguise: Nested Meditations to Delight the Mind and Awaken the Soul,* which introduced this new writing form. The repetition and surprising shifts that are part of the nested form mirror something about how the routines of daily married life can surprise us with grace and deeper meaning. Second, near the end of each chapter you'll find a "To Have and to Laugh" page. We all need comic relief—a little reward after considering lots of new ideas about marriage. Third, a "Key Summary Points" page follows the "To Have and to Laugh" and overviews the main ideas covered in the chapter. Fourth, each chapter concludes with questions for couple or small group discussion.

The appendices contain material for couples who want to soak up every last bit of what this book has to offer their marriages. Included are a sampling of marriage research (Appendix A), a list marital of toxins to avoid (Appendix B), an extended example of empathic listening (Appendix C), and a section on how some people resist the concept of extraordinary marriage (Appendix D).

So read on and start learning about the practices you can use to make your marriage extraordinary. You have the rest of your lives to understand and live them more fully. My hope is that *The Seven Spiritual Practices of Marriage* helps you create a more committed, intimate, passionate, spiritual relationship based on deep and daily honoring.

NAMASTE MARRIAGE SELF-ASSESSMENT

This tool may help you prioritize your work on the seven spiritual practices of marriage. Each partner separately rate the seven statements below using the following scale:

1	2	3	4	5	6
Strongly Disagree	Disagree	Slightly Disagree	Slightly Agree	Agree	Strongly Agree

HER
RATING

HIS
RATING

_____   1. We share a clear vision for the kind of marriage we want to create.   _____

_____   2. We feel connected with each other almost every day of our relationship.   _____

_____   3. We handle conflicts in an honoring manner.   _____

_____   4. We accept and affirm each other "as is."   _____

_____   5. We each work on personal growth to become better individuals and marriage partners.   _____

_____   6. Our sexual expression of married love is mutually-satisfying and life-giving.   _____

_____   7. We experience our relationship as a spiritual companionship that reveals God's presence in our daily lives.   _____

Determine which areas you both rated in the "disagree" range or in which areas your answers did not correspond (one of you said "agree," the other said "disagree.") Consider focusing on these practices first. (Each question number above corresponds to the practice, e.g. question #5 corresponds to practice #5.)

In the artist's portrayal of Create a shared vision, *the pyramid represents the common dream of marriage crafted by the partners, who are symbolized by the eyes on either side. The pyramid rests on rock (solid foundation), yet it is clear that the pyramid has shifted (a couple's vision may change as the marriage progresses). On the cover (or page 14), the pyramid appears to have been dropped in a pond and ripples out to the other six practices.*

CREATE A SHARED VISION

SUMMARY OF THIS PRACTICE

Create a shared vision is about making sure you and your partner build your marriage on solid rock by meeting regularly to discuss your marital vision. Doing this will strengthen your commitment and reveal the wonderful things that can happen when you become intentional about turning your individual and shared dreams into realities. You can create a great marriage if you commit to regular meetings to stay clear on what you both envision for your life together and follow through with action.

SPIRITUAL FOCUS
FOR THIS PRACTICE

The rain fell, the floods came, and the winds blew and buffeted the house. But it did not collapse; it had been set solidly on rock.

Matthew 7:25

After my father died a difficult and unexpected death in 2002, Claudia suggested we increase our once-a-week marriage meetings to every day for a while to help me work through the grief. What began as a response to losing Dad evolved into a beautiful commitment to our marriage. Three years later, we still meet five days per week at 7:00 a.m. after our children get on the school bus. We talk and dream about various aspects of our life together. These meetings have been a hidden gold mine for our marriage. Our return on the investment of about four hours per week has been enormous.

Wait, don't put this book down yet! I'm not recommending that every couple meet five days per week. I am, however, strongly suggesting that you commit to some kind of plan for regular meetings—once per week, even once per month if that's where you want to begin. Any amount of time you invest in creating a shared vision will pay wonderful and surprising dividends. Marital visioning is central to creating a Namaste marriage.

I call this approach to meeting and planning life together *intentional*. The idea is that a great marriage is created on purpose by two people committed to filling their life together with loving behaviors that lead to deep and lasting feelings of love. This is completely different from the model that portrays love (or being in love) as primarily a feeling that leads people to treat each other well. That familiar model is not intentional—it assumes that the feeling of love will carry the day. As Aaron Beck wrote in *Love is Never Enough*, marriage is far more than hoping that the feeling of being in love persists. For many couples, loving feelings do not persist because the partners have not learned to be intentional about creating a relationship filled with daily loving behaviors.

A woman and man stand up publicly on their wedding day and profess lifelong commitment to one another. In our culture, we celebrate the sacred and bold nature of this commitment,

A vision comes in advance of any task well done.

KATHERINE LOGAN

I know of no more encouraging fact than the unquestionable ability of man to elevate his life by a conscious endeavor.

HENRY DAVID THOREAU

often in grand style. Beyond the wedding, however, we don't have clear ideas about how this commitment is lived out in a marriage on a day-to-day basis. Have you ever heard the saying, "If you don't know where you're going, you probably won't get there"? This statement is as true in marriage as anywhere else. Most ordinary marriages operate on unspoken assumptions about how married life should be. Conflict arises when the assumptions of the partners turn out to be different, which is almost always the case. After finding it too difficult to discuss these unconscious assumptions, many couples learn to just keep quiet and lower their expectations. An extraordinary, Namaste marriage requires a more intentional approach.

People change and forget to tell each other.

LILLIAN HELLMAN

Do you know any leader who tries to run a business without ever having meetings to focus on the company's vision, goals, plans, and results? Not likely. Why do we try to run our marriages without such meetings? You and your partner are the co-executive officers of your marriage operation. *Create a shared vision* involves making a commitment to meet periodically to ensure that you're leading your marriage in the same direction.

Creating a shared vision isn't like learning to ride a bike, which once accomplished never needs to be done again. It is more like pedaling the bike. If we stop pedaling, the bike will eventually cease moving forward and will fall over. If we stop visioning in our marriages, they cease moving forward and may fall over too.

Marital visioning, then, is a process more than a product. The easiest guarantee to offer a newly married couple is that the vision they start out with will not be the one they end up with. In a Namaste marriage, the vision changes as the couple grows older, but it remains a mutually-determined map for a committed, intimate, passionate, and spiritual life together.

As I compared the happily married couples with thousands of divorcing couples I have seen in the past twenty-five years, it was clear that these men and women had early on created a firm basis for their relationship and had continued to build it together . . . The happy couples regarded their marriage as a work in progress that needed continued attention lest it fall into disrepair.

JUDITH WALLERSTEIN

Nested Meditation

Do you have the time?

Do you have the time
of your life?

Do you have the time
of your life
or does someone else perhaps?

Do you have the time
of your life
or does someone else? Perhaps
it's later than you think.

Marital visioning is not just about discussing what you want your future to be like. More importantly, it's about getting clear on what you want your life now to be like. Each day of your life together is a gift, and you never know which will be your last. There's no time like the present to begin envisioning and creating the marriage you really want!

PRACTICING
CREATE A SHARED VISION
IN YOUR MARRIAGE

DECIDE TO BUILD A NAMASTE MARRIAGE

The decision to build a Namaste marriage, like your wedding vows, needs to be reaffirmed regularly throughout your marriage if it is to remain a guiding force in your life. Deciding to create an extraordinary marriage is an ongoing practice, not a one-time event.

Your life is shaped by the end you live for.

THOMAS MERTON

☞ Discuss the statement on page 32. Don't sign it too quickly. It represents a significant commitment of time and energy. Even one hour per week for fifty years is over 2500 hours! If you do decide to sign it, consider copying it and taping the signed agreement to your bathroom mirror, your refrigerator, or somewhere else where you'll see it frequently until you establish a reliable habit of meeting regularly.

If one or both of you are experiencing some resistance to the idea of making your marriage extraordinary, read and discuss appendix D, "Resistance to Creating an Extraordinary Marriage."

> ## *Let's Go for an Extraordinary Marriage!*
>
> As your partner, I agree to continue learning and growing with you throughout our marriage. I commit to the process of creating a truly extraordinary marriage with you. I will honor and love you by remaining true to the commitment to meet periodically to discuss the kind of marriage we want. I will make my best effort to follow through with action on the life we envision so that our marital dreams can become realities.
>
> _____   _____
>
> Wife   Husband
>
> Date: _____   Date: _____

HOLD REGULAR VISIONING MEETINGS

For several years Claudia and I felt frustrated that our vegetable garden didn't produce much worthy of being eaten. By late summer it was typically overgrown with weeds. Because it was a good distance away from the house, it rarely received any water beyond what nature gave. Recently, Claudia suggested that we begin some organic gardens. We hauled in several truckloads of rich, dark soil and made new gardens closer to the house. We enjoyed watering those gardens regularly. What grew from our work was a delight! We had zucchinis, tomatoes, broccoli, kale, lettuce, and many other delicious vegetables growing like they were on steroids. All it took was a bed of rich soil, planting the seeds, occasional weeding, and regular watering.

The greatest achievement was at first and for a time a dream. The oak sleeps in the acorn . . . and in the highest vision of the soul, a waking angel stirs. Dreams are the seedlings of realities . . .

JAMES ALLEN

A marriage is like a garden. If we give it time and attention, the seeds we plant grow strong and bear much fruit. If we fail to invest time and energy in our marriages, they will disappoint us at best and will likely become choked with weeds.

Visioning meetings create in a marriage a rich bed of what Benjamin and Roz Zander in *The Art of Possibility* have called "possibility thinking." These consistent meetings will allow you to plant new seeds and discuss weeding out whatever is hindering the growth of your marriage. Visioning meetings refresh a marriage with the "water" of quiet, focused reflection and produce a bountiful harvest as you follow through with your plans.

The most common objection to marital visioning meetings is, "We just don't have the time." If you want a fruitful and rewarding marriage, you don't have the time *not* to have these meetings. If your marriage is truly among the most important things in your life, there is no question that you can find time for these meetings. For couples just beginning the marital visioning process, I often suggest meeting once a week for an hour. This is .59% of your week. In contrast, if you are typical, you give about 30% of your week to work, 33% to sleep, and about 12% to watching television. I am certain you can give 1/20th of the time that the average adult spends watching television to creating a vision for your marriage. Simply turning the television off for certain blocks of time could create space for you to begin looking at the kind of marriage you want. If young children make it difficult to find space, be creative about how to keep them occupied for one hour per week. If they are old enough to understand, tell them what you're doing and expect them to respect your desire to nurture your relationship. Modeling that kind of commitment to your marriage is one of the best gifts you can give your children.

Even if you begin by meeting only once a month for an hour, you'll have twelve more hours per year of intentional focus on the kind of marriage you want to create than you had before. Once you get into the process, however, I think you'll realize that the direction of growth is putting more time into the process, not less.

Television has proved that people will look at anything rather than each other.

ANN LANDERS

Whatever you can do or dream you can, begin it. Boldness has genius, power, and magic in it.

GOETHE

Love does not consist in gazing at each other, but in looking outward together in the same direction.

ANTOINE DE SAINT-EXUPERY

⚷ Take ten minutes to complete and discuss the brief form below.

Do I think visioning meetings would be good for our marriage? _____

Do I want to commit to such meetings? _____

Would I be more comfortable if we tried several such meetings and then re-evaluated their usefulness? _____

If we decide to commit to a set of trial meetings or to ongoing meetings, when could we realistically make time for the meetings?

Best day of the week: _____

Best time of day: _____

Frequency of meetings: _____

Length of meetings: _____

Date we will start: _____

If you can get a first visioning meeting in your calendars, you've taken a big step toward building your marriage on solid rock. Treat that meeting time as a high priority and do not schedule other commitments over it.

Guidelines for Positive Visioning Meetings

Love is often a fruit of marriage.

MOLIERE

If you decide to begin having visioning meetings—and I hope that you do—it is important to make sure these meetings are enjoyable and positive in tone. Here are some guidelines for making sure that's the case:

◆ Make the meetings a time of connection. Be sure you have privacy and quiet. Meet in a pleasant space and consider sharing coffee, tea, dessert or any other simple pleasure that helps define the meeting as a time of warmth and intimacy.

◆ Consider beginning each meeting with a prayer, a statement of affirmation for each other, a warm hug, or the Namaste greeting (see page 192). The goal of beginning this way is to make it clear from the start that your desire is for the meeting to stay grounded in positive, honoring energy.

◆ Maintain some kind of physical contact during the meeting (hold hands, sit knee-to-knee, or sit on a couch together so that your legs are in contact). This physical touch is a potent sign throughout the meeting of your desire to make it a time for honoring and closeness. If conflict begins to arise in a meeting, use the power of honoring touch to keep the tension from escalating.

◆ At the beginning of each meeting, talk about how you want to spend the time. Taking a few minutes to set an agenda will help the meetings stay focused.

◆ Bring a notebook and your planner or calendar to the meeting so that you can write down any action steps and who will carry them out.

If you follow these guidelines, your visioning meetings will feel connecting, even exciting, as you intentionally create your life together. If, however, you allow the meetings to be primarily a place for conflict, one or both of you will begin avoiding them.

WHAT TO DO IN YOUR FIRST VISIONING MEETING

The most important agenda for your first meeting or two is to brainstorm all of the areas that you would like to vision about together. Write them down in a notebook that you will bring to each of your meetings. Later you can sort through the brainstorm of ideas and gather the items into groups. The box on the next page contains some categories under which your brainstormed ideas might fall.

Everything that is great in life is the product of slow growth.

WILLIAM JORDAN

SOME ELEMENTS OF A SHARED MARITAL VISION

1. **Values:** What is most important in your life?
2. **Spirituality:** The role of faith, prayer, church attendance, and spirituality in your marriage.
3. **Finances:** Guiding principles for managing your money (spending habits, saving, future planning, charity).
4. **Emotional closeness:** Your vision for keeping healthy emotional intimacy and communication.
5. **Intellectual growth and conversation:** Reading, learning, conversing on topics of mutual interest.
6. **Affection:** Your vision for maintaining physical intimacy (day-to-day affection).
7. **Dating:** How often, where, who plans, expense.
8. **Romance and sex:** A shared vision for keeping passion strong.
9. **Conflict:** A vision or model for dealing with conflict.
10. **Family:** Your vision for family life (if you have or hope to have children).
11. **Work:** Balancing work and marriage/family; making work life fulfilling.
12. **Meals:** How often to eat together as a couple/family.
13. **Friendships:** Your vision for supporting healthy one-on-one and couple friendships.
14. **Male and female roles in marriage:** Who does what?
15. **Relating to extended family:** Your vision for family-of-origin and in-law relationships.
16. **Vacations/getaways/travel/adventure:** How often, where, expense?
17. **Health:** Exercise, nutrition, and sleep.
18. **Where to live:** Geographic location and type of home.
19. **Home organization/cleanliness, décor or remodeling:** How you want your home to look.
20. **Your orientation to the larger culture:** Where you will flow with the culture and where you will stand firm against it.
21. **Individual dreams:** Supporting one another's individual life dreams.
22. **Service:** How your lives and your marriage can benefit others.
23. **Retirement:** Your vision for later years.
24. **Other visioning topics of your choosing.**

The list of possible visioning topics is endless. You can vision about the upcoming holidays, the orchard you want to plant in the back yard, where your kids go to school, how to celebrate your twenty-fifth wedding anniversary, how much money to give to charity, how to handle phone calls at dinner, what to do about a difficult family relationship, and on and on.

Once you have brainstormed a list of agenda items, subsequent meetings focus on these items in whatever order you feel makes sense.

> 🔑 Review the sample brainstorm list on page 36. Decide which items to include in your marital visioning brainstorm, but don't just use this list. It's important that your visioning process be of your own creation, not something out of a book. Try creating a series of present-tense statements about your marriage (such as, "We go on dates regularly" or "We touch affectionately every day") to clarify your vision.

FOLLOWING THROUGH WITH ACTION

A great vision is powerless to help you create the marriage you both want if it isn't translated into action. In fact, if you meet and talk about wonderful and creative ideas and there is little follow through, the whole exercise may prove more disillusioning than uplifting.

For many years, I was a rather disorganized person. One of my first jobs as a psychologist was director of a mental health center. I remember the day I received a call from another center's director that I had forgotten about an important lunch meeting. That day I realized I could no longer operate by my old style. Life was prodding me to get more organized. That's when I began using a planner with a daily place to list action items. That tool—which costs me about seven cents per day—has made

The best way to predict your future is to create it.
STEPHEN COVEY

Anything less than a conscious commitment to the important is an unconscious commitment to the unimportant.
STEPHEN COVEY

a huge difference in my ability to follow through on my own goals and on what I tell other people I will do.

Claudia and I both bring our planners to our visioning meetings. If we're dreaming about a horseback riding trip in two months, one of us needs to take responsibility to write down "research horse trip" in our planner. Otherwise, that good idea will get lost in the swirl of other activities. Some of our meeting time is actually devoted to just making sure we both know about all the events coming up in our lives, which requires a comparison of planners.

> ⚷ Bring a planner or notebook to every visioning meeting so that you can write down any ideas and clarify who (one or both of you) will take any required action steps. Review your notes during your next meeting and determine if the necessary action steps were taken. This process will allow you to continue moving forward on creating the marriage you envision.

HOW TO KEEP VISIONING MEETINGS INTERESTING

The most basic principle in psychology is that people repeat behaviors they experience as rewarding and avoid those they find distasteful, boring, or otherwise unrewarding. Be willing to experiment with different times, formats, frequencies, topics, or activities to ensure that the marital visioning process is a positive experience for your marriage. Make the meetings enjoyable so that you will both look forward to them.

One way to make visioning meetings something you'll want to return to again and again is to link them with what you already enjoy. Here are some ideas:

Life shrinks or expands in proportion to one's courage.

ANAIS NIN

◆ Share a meal while discussing your vision (or before or after).

◆ Read quietly, then discuss what you have read to begin your meeting.

◆ Write love letters and then read them to each other—see 20/20 exercise, page 65).

◆ Be affectionate (hold hands, embrace, give massages).

◆ Meet before going out on a date together (let the baby-sitter watch the children during your meeting).

◆ Pray together (to begin or end meeting).

◆ Make love before or after the visioning meeting.

Be sure, however, not to clutter the meeting up with too many other activities. The idea is to really focus on discussing where you are in your marriage and where you want to go. Make sure that you differentiate your visioning meetings from typical "date" time. Visioning meetings are more intentional and focused than going out to "talk things over." Dating time is important, but it is typically not focused enough to allow for effective visioning.

If you find that you end up in conflict when you have marital visioning meetings, it is probably more important for you to work on practices #2 and #3 first (*Make connection the norm* and *Bring honoring to conflict*). Don't give up on visioning meetings if they initially produce tension. Learning to play the guitar hurt my fingers for the first several weeks. Pushing through that initial discomfort led to a lifetime of enjoyment.

Ideals are like stars: you will not succeed in touching them with your hands, but like the seafaring man on the desert of waters, you choose them as your guides, and following them you reach your destiny.

CARL SCHURZ

> ⚷ Begin a visioning meeting with ten minutes of shared meditation or brief massage. This can establish honoring, peaceful energy prior to your discussion.

MARITAL VISIONING: FOUR GUIDING PRINCIPLES

You and your partner can create whatever vision you choose as you remain faithful to meeting periodically throughout your marriage. The four principles in this section are included to help you make sure your vision is not limited by culturally-determined ideas of "how life is" that can prevent you from seeing deeper and more connected ways to envision and live out your marriage.

Visioning Principle #1
BE A BOULDER IN THE TORRENT OF THE CULTURE

A Namaste marriage cannot be created by accepting our secular culture's idea of what a marriage should be. The culture's model is the blueprint for ordinary or troubled marriages. Because you are reading this book, I assume you are aiming higher.

Here is an image that may help you visualize how difficult it is to prioritize marriage in a culture that tells us to consider money, work, or physical appearances most important. A few years ago, our family spent two weeks camping in Great Smoky Mountain National Park. We were able to get a campsite right on the Little River, a swiftly flowing mountain stream full of rocks and boulders. For a week and a half we had clear weather, but on the evening of the eleventh day it began to pour. The rain came down in sheets all night long. Upon emerging from the camper in the morning, we were greeted by the sights and sounds of a white wall of water, a torrent both beautiful and frightening! The river had risen so much that it was raging uncomfortably close to our camper. I instinctively put my arms behind me to hold back our one-year-old son, though he was still sleeping peacefully in the camper. If he or any of us had fallen into that torrent, we would have been swept away instantly.

To know what you prefer instead of humbly saying Amen to what the world tells you you ought to prefer, is to have kept your soul alive.

ROBERT LOUIS STEVENSON

As I took in that scene, I focused on the largest boulder in the middle of the stream. All of the smaller rocks were under water, but this giant was holding its ground as the river slammed into it with all its power. That boulder had been there for thousands of years, seen countless storms come and go, and had never budged an inch.

One could take the boulder in Little River as a metaphor for stubbornness or rigidity. I think of it, though, as a wonderful symbol for the kind of strength it takes to create a deeply spiritual marriage in a culture that is in every moment tempting us to focus on surface gratification. In our society, one cannot turn on the television or radio or read a newspaper or magazine without encountering an advertisement designed to maximize our desires. We swim so constantly in materialism that it becomes difficult to realize how deeply this torrent of messages affects our worldview and our relationships.

Slow down and enjoy life. It's not only the scenery you miss by going too fast—you also miss the sense of where you are going and why.

EDDIE CANTOR

In a world preoccupied with having, succeeding, and becoming wealthy, relationships do not receive top priority. In a Namaste marriage, they do. You may be thinking, *Yes, I believe relationships with God and loved ones are the most important things in life,* but living that way consistently—backing up our words with intentional actions—is challenging.

If you are to create an extraordinary marriage, you must define where you will hold your ground like the boulder in Little River rather than let the torrent of the culture wash your relationship away. A Namaste marriage is necessarily countercultural because our society is not conducive to women and men experiencing the best that marriage has to offer.

Another way of thinking about being a boulder in the torrent is developing a spirituality of time. Many people don't have the time of their life in marriage because they never really *have* the time of their life. By this I mean that people do not enjoy themselves as much as they could, because they live as if their time is not their own. They feel driven along by demands, rarely giving the important things in life the time they deserve.

The trouble with being in the rat race is that even if you win, you're still a rat.

LILY TOMLIN

Time is the raw material of our lives. The way we spend our time is an ongoing statement about what we consider most important. Failing to create a spirituality of time leaves us with the "default" option, which in our culture is busyness coupled with a sense of time shortage. This makes it very difficult to allocate sufficient time to what we say matters most.

How you manage your time is crucial to the quality of your marriage and family (if you have children). As a marriage counselor, sometimes it seems that almost every couple I see starts our first meeting with, "We're so busy that we have very little time just for us."

Paul Pearsall coined the term "marriage investment minutes" (MIMs). His idea was that a marriage is similar to a financial investment. If we put a small amount of money in an account, we are not surprised that the monthly statement indicates we've received a small return on the investment. Likewise, if we invest little time and energy (few MIMs) in our marriage, it should be no shock that the marriage does not thrive. That's like expecting a $10 investment to return $1000.

Willard Harley, author of *His Needs, Her Needs,* has said he believes a good marriage requires about fifteen hours per week of quality couple time. I like the boldness of his proclamation in a culture that unceasingly promotes the illusion of time famine.

The main thing is to keep the main thing the main thing.
STEPHEN COVEY

☞ Write down how many MIMs you currently invest in your relationship per day or per week. Then write down how many you think would be necessary to experience your marriage at its best. Talk with each other about how you can move closer to investing the time your marriage needs to thrive.

☞ To make this be-a-boulder idea concrete, consider writing a brief statement together which captures your orientation toward the culture. Your statement may be a single sentence or phrase ("Think countercultural") or a long treatise. It doesn't matter, but what does matter is that you realize that flowing with the culture in every respect will not allow you to create an extraordinary marriage.

Visioning Principle #2

KEEP FIRST THINGS FIRST

One aspect of the importance of being countercultural deserves special attention. Today work/relationship balance has joined money and sex as the issues that married couples fight about most. If you're not talking openly about balance, there's a good chance at least one person in your marriage is concerned about it. A better guide for our individual, marital, and family health than a work ethic is a balance ethic—the combination of the three main activities of life: work, relationship, and leisure.

A friend once shared with me that he always believed his priorities were God first, family second, and work third. That was until he arrived home from work one day and found his bags packed on the front doorstep. After passing through a difficult time in his marriage, he came to see that he had been mostly giving lip service to the God-family-work ordering of priorities. In reality, his priorities had been: work first and everything else a distant second.

Stephen Covey uses an effective visual image for the importance of keeping first things first. Our lives, he says, are like jars filled up with small rocks—the many day-to-day responsibilities that we all have. Because our time is finite, we can only fit so much into the "jar" of each day, and often the biggest rocks—what we say are the most important things in our lives—don't make it into the jar. Covey's simple yet profound idea is to put the big rocks in the jar first. That means determining what is most important to you and putting it in your calendar or planner first. Even if you do this, you will still, as Covey says, need to "exercise integrity at the moment of choice." By this he means honoring your commitment to big rocks when other involvements try to pressure you to schedule over them.

I grew up in a family with a strong work ethic, but I discovered, in my life and in working with thousands of clients, that a work ethic is not a sufficient guide for one's life. I still remember our six-year-old daughter Emily refusing the money I was offering her for having completed her Saturday chores. "I don't want

In every study in which Americans are asked what they value most in assessing the quality of their lives, marriage comes first—ahead of friends, job, and money.

JUDITH WALLERSTEIN
AND SANDRA BLAKESLEE

Balancing is a discipline precisely because the act of giving something up is painful … I learned, however, that the loss of balance is ultimately more painful than the giving up required to maintain balance.

M. SCOTT PECK

43

If you were to pause and think seriously about the "first things" in your life— the three or four things that matter most—what would they be? Are these things receiving the care, emphasis, and time you really want to give them?

STEPHEN COVEY

your money, Dad," she said—"I want your time." Most of us have Emilies in our lives that need more of our time and energy. Sometimes our Emilies are important people; sometimes they are dreams we have been neglecting that call out to us periodically, "I just want some of your time!"

Just like riding a bicycle, the moment you stop working to keep your balance in marriage, you begin to lose it. Few couples openly and regularly discuss the balance between work, relationship, and leisure in their marriages. If you address balance in your visioning meetings, your chances for creating an extraordinary marriage are much higher.

This book is primarily about marriage, yet most married couples eventually make the transition to family. A married couple, the co-leaders of the family, is responsible for determining the "family culture" or setting the tone for "how we do things in this family." Keeping first things first means creating a vision that allows your family life to thrive rather than just to survive or struggle along without sufficient direction. But that is another book!

A balance ethic is the combination of a work ethic, a relationship ethic, and a leisure ethic. Try making three columns in a notebook as follows:

WORK ETHIC | RELATIONSHIP ETHIC | LEISURE ETHIC

Under each column, list your guiding principles for that part of life. Make sure the ideas are specific and measurable. Instead of writing, "Spend time with my children" under "relationship ethic," try something more specific such as, "Spend fifteen minutes nightly reading to my daughter."

Under "leisure ethic" include ideas about the five kinds of leisure: *recreation* (fun), *creation* (hobbies or other creative outlets), *relaxation* (nonproductive time), *rejuvenation* (behaviors to replenish body and spirit, such as sleep and exercise), and *reflection* (prayer, reading, journaling).

> ⚷ Write down the five biggest rocks in your life. Discuss what you wrote with your partner. Then follow through with scheduling time for these top priorities in your planner or calendar. This is how to keep first things first: Block out time in advance for what you say is most important in your life.

Visioning Principle #3

Nurture Three Sets of Dreams

Many wedding services use the ritual of lighting a candle to symbolize the union that occurs on that special day. I've seen this ceremony performed two ways. The more common way is for the bride's and the groom's parents to start a match from two separate candles, light the marriage candle by joining the flames together, and then blow out the first two candles. This symbolizes "the two shall become one." Occasionally I've seen the individual candles left burning after the marriage candle is lit. I prefer the symbolism of this latter approach because it conveys that the union of the couple adds to, but does not snuff out, the individual spirits and dreams of those choosing to travel through life together.

Put another way, just because you light my fire doesn't mean you get to blow out my candle! And if you try to, I'll be like one of those trick birthday candles that keeps relighting! A great marriage shines brightly in part because it respects that the partners who make it up want to shine their best individual selves into the world too.

An important part of keeping a marriage full of life is learning how to honor your dreams, my dreams, and our dreams. Creating an extraordinary marriage is a wonderful dream, but it is not the only dream in life. Some joint dreams, such as raising a family or starting a business together, are intertwined with

If you have built castles in the air, your work need not be lost; that is where they should be. Now put foundations under them.

Henry David Thoreau

Go confidently in the direction of your dreams! Live the life you've imagined.

Henry David Thoreau

the marriage but go beyond the one-on-one relationship of the couple. Individual career or other dreams are rarely the same for both partners. He may want to be a painter, she may want to become an expert on organic gardening. These do not need to be shared dreams.

Healthy people, whether married or not, pursue dreams that give their individual journeys to God depth and purpose. If couples overemphasize the common dream (our dream), individual dreams can get lost or overshadowed. Discussion of individual dreams can be incorporated into your marital visioning meetings. Truly supporting your partner as an individual will paradoxically create a much more joyful and interconnected marriage.

Many men go fishing all of their lives without knowing that it is not fish they are after.

HENRY DAVID THOREAU

> One way to get a clear view of your own and your partner's dreams is for each of you to put the phrase "Life List" on the top of a sheet of paper and then write down all the things you want to do or experience before you die. Talk with each other about your life lists. Which ones appear to be "low hanging fruit," ready to be picked if you become intentional about them?

Visioning Principle #4
KEEP IT CLEAN

On the way back from a trip to Yellowstone National Park, one of our daughters developed severe diarrhea from giardia, a bacteria from the urine of wild animals that runs off into mountain lakes and streams. The seventeen-hundred-mile trip home was made much longer by the need to stop for bathroom breaks along the side of the road every twenty miles or so! It's amazing how an invisible organism in a small swallow of lake water could wreak such havoc on our little girl's health.

Unchecked toxic behavior patterns can ravage your marriage's health just the way giardia threatened our daughter's. A decision to create a Namaste marriage is also a commitment to eliminate behaviors that can poison the marriage you're trying to keep alive and growing.

Imagine if this were a book on getting your body into an extraordinary state of health. There would be lots of suggestions about what to do—especially about how to exercise and eat right. There would also be plenty about what not to do: Don't eat too much saturated fat, don't drink too much alcohol, don't do drugs, don't smoke, don't eat too much sugar, and so on. Just as keeping our bodies fit requires a commitment to avoid certain foods and behaviors, creating an extraordinary marriage includes avoiding marital toxins—the behaviors that can poison a relationship, sometimes quickly, sometimes with a slow buildup of poisons over time.

I hold to the doctrine that with ordinary talent, and extraordinary perseverance, all things are attainable.

THOMAS BUXTON

Appendix B contains information about avoiding fifteen marital toxins. If negative behaviors are poisoning your marriage, please review the appendix, make every effort to eliminate the behaviors, and seek professional help if necessary.

☞ Read "The Story of Ella and Sam" on the next page. Then review the various toxic behaviors listed in Appendix B (p. 208). Discuss whether you ever witnessed one or more of the problem behaviors in the home in which you grew up. Decide to ban such behaviors from your relationship or to go for professional help if you are not successful getting rid of them on your own.

THE STORY OF ELLA AND SAM

When Ella and Sam met, a wonderful elixir of natural chemicals filled their bloodstreams and let them experience the high that we call "falling in love." They married while still on that high but were slightly disillusioned when the love chemicals receded to normal levels. Even as they enjoyed the first years of their marriage, small amounts of a particular toxin began to seep silently into their life together. Their marriage started to get sick.

The symptoms were subtle at first—less conversation, fewer nights out together, arguments over money. Eventually, as the mysterious toxin multiplied in their marriage, the illness took a turn for the worse.

Ella got sick and tired of Sam getting home late from work. Sam got sick and tired of the angry way she told him this again and again. Ella got sick and tired of Sam's lack of affection. Sam got sick and tired of Ella's headaches. They began sleeping in separate beds, rationalizing it at first as a way to deal with Sam's snoring. Their relationship drifted slowly apart, and when conflict came up they either ignored it or fought mean-spiritedly about it. They spent days after most fights giving each other the cold shoulder.

Finally they went to a counselor. After talking with them, the counselor solved the mystery of the unidentified toxin. She told them: "The bad news is that you two have developed a bad case of Sam and Ella poisoning. The good news is that each of you, by the way you honor the other and commit yourself to learning a deeper way to love, has the power to treat the illness and restore your marriage to superb health."

To Have and to Laugh

Got Vision?

Mr. Cow: Oh, honey, I'd love to meet with you to discuss our dreams. I'm envisioning another twenty years of grazing day after day, just hoping to avoid the meat grinder as long as possible? How about you?

Mrs. Cow: What?! Grazing for twenty more years?! I've been having these strange dreams about a cat and a fiddle and a dish and a spoon and a cow jumping over the moon!

Key Summary Points
CREATE A SHARED VISION

◆ Make a commitment to creating an extraordinary, Namaste marriage.

◆ Meet regularly throughout your marriage to discuss your relationship, dreams, lifestyle, communication, sexuality, and whatever else you choose to put on your agenda.

◆ In your first meeting or two, brainstorm all the agenda items you want to talk about in your ongoing meetings. Discuss the agenda items in your subsequent meetings.

◆ Bring a notebook or planner to each meeting so that you can remember and write down what you discussed and who agreed to be responsible for taking action.

◆ Keep your visioning meetings alive and interesting (see page 39).

◆ As you form your marital vision, decide where to take a stand against aspects of the culture that do not support a strong marriage.

◆ Develop the practice of identifying what is most important to you and scheduling time in your calendars for those priorities. Strive to keep work, family and leisure in balance. This will allow you to keep first things first in your life together.

◆ Make sure your marital vision supports the individual dreams of both partners.

◆ Discuss the toxic behaviors in Appendix B that have great power to undermine the beautiful relationship you want to build. Eliminate any of those behaviors that may be present in your relationship or get professional help if they persist.

DISCUSSION QUESTIONS

1. An extraordinary marriage is one in which both partners go 1) beyond the ordinary by committing to intentional behaviors that build a strong relationship and 2) beneath the ordinary to see the sacredness and deeper meaning of daily life. Does this vision of marriage appeal to you? Do you believe it is possible?

2. This book states that meeting regularly with your partner to create a shared vision for your marriage is a key commitment for building a great marriage. Why do you think so few married couples do this? What are the obstacles that could keep you or other couples from being faithful to such meetings?

3. The four guiding principles for creating a shared vision presented in the chapter are:

   ◆ Be a boulder in the torrent—determine where you will hold firm against the flow of the secular culture;
   ◆ Keep first things first—develop a clear sense of priorities and give time to what you say is most important;
   ◆ Nurture three sets of dreams—support her, his, and our dreams;
   ◆ Keep it clean—make sure that toxic behaviors have no place in your marriage.

   Which of the four principles do you think is most important and why?

The artist chose a dove to represent the peace that daily connection brings to a marriage. The interlocking connections just below the bird are "dovetail" joints used in woodworking to bind pieces together durably. The numbers represent a calendar and the daily nature of Make connection the norm. *The circular, swirling symbol is a depiction of the connection of masculine and feminine in marriage.*

2

MAKE CONNECTION
THE NORM

SUMMARY OF THIS PRACTICE

Creating a Namaste marriage requires a commitment to daily connection. This means that the interaction of the partners is marked by warm greetings, plenty of affection, and words that are respectfully chosen and spoken in an honoring way. *Make connection the norm* is the spiritual practice of committing to the behaviors that, over time, make the difference between a close marriage and a distant or troubled one. Make sure affection and connection are the rule and disconnection and conflict are the exception in your marriage.

SPIRITUAL FOCUS
FOR THIS PRACTICE

*I will never forget you. I have carved
you on the palms of my hands.*

Isaiah 49:16

When we talk about good marriages, we often say things like, "They look like they were just married!" What we mean is that the couple still shows clear evidence of being warm, loving, and connected with each other. It may seem almost too basic to point out that married couples should strive to be kind and honoring to one another every day. *Make connection the norm* involves maintaining an awareness that kindness and affection are the way things should be daily instead of allowing chronic conflict or distance to make you believe that marriage is essentially an everyday pain!

Namaste marriages are unusually connected. This means both partners are constantly aware of the presence or absence of a feeling of being in sync or on track with one another. When the connection is there, it signals that things are going smoothly. When the connection is not there, it's time to find out why. Connection is expressed and felt in the kind and tender words and behaviors that spouses exchange. Spontaneous hugs, kisses, touches, massages, affirmations, surprises, simple acts of kindness—these are some of the ways that couples communicate, "We are connected; things are good between us."

When counselors first see a couple, it's often after years of the partners drifting through their days with little or no sign of connection. At one time they dreamed of "endless love," but now they seem resigned to just living under the same roof. I remember asking one couple to hold hands in my office. They extended their hands awkwardly as if they were afraid the other had just come down with the plague!

In ordinary marriages, connection may come or go, but there is no norm that it be there daily as an indicator of marital health. In troubled relationships, the couple often has forgotten altogether the importance of daily monitoring of connection. Many couples become habituated to this situation, thinking that it's just the way marriage is once you get past the first few months or years.

Chains do not hold a marriage together. It is threads, hundreds of tiny threads, which sew people together through the years.

SIMONE SIGNORET

When you decide to make connection the norm and disconnection the exception, you will eventually become aware much more quickly when a problem in the marriage needs resolving. The lack of connection will signal that there is unresolved tension in the air. The desire to get back to a peaceful feeling of connection will motivate you to use the conflict resolution skills presented in practice #3 (*Bring honoring to conflict*).

The intentional model of marriage is based on the truth that if we want something to happen, we need to take steps to make it happen. Being intentional about daily connection means agreeing on how often you expect certain signs or words of connection, such as hugs, thank-you's, or other indicators of basic honoring. The contrast between a couple that is intentional about daily connection and a couple that makes no particular effort to ensure daily connection is like the difference between a car that is regularly serviced and one that is never maintained. Both will run for a while, but the latter is far more likely to break down.

Joy does not reside in some future world. It sits across the table from you, needing only your undivided attention.

WILLIAM MARTIN

Nested Meditation

Many years I waited.

Many years I waited
for bluebirds to show up.

Many years I waited
for bluebirds to show, uplifting me with their plumage.

Many years I waited.
For bluebirds to show, up-
lifting me with their plumage,
I had only to build them a home.

This meditation was inspired by building a bluebird house, putting it up in the back yard, and being amazed as a pair of bluebirds moved in the very next day! I hadn't seen a bluebird on our property for seven years, but as soon as I made a home for them, they seemed to appear out of nowhere. They were, of course, there all along. Intimacy in marriage is like those bluebirds—waiting for us to build it a home, which we do by keeping our marriages affectionate, honoring, and connected on a daily basis.

> ## PRACTICING
> ### *MAKE CONNECTION THE NORM*
> ### IN YOUR MARRIAGE

SHARE EACH OTHER'S LIFE INTERESTS

Whereas women are more likely to define intimacy as *sharing feelings* or talking about things, many men tend to think of closeness as *doing things together,* particularly activities in which they are highly interested. This means that when a woman makes an effort to spend time with her husband doing something he deeply enjoys, he is likely to feel closer to her. Surely, women enjoy their husbands taking an interest in their activities too, but they are not as likely as men to define this as the core of intimacy.

While most of the other ideas in this chapter for creating daily connection concern ways of *communicating* love and affection to one another, it is important to remember that *doing things together* is a primary way that some people experience a sense of connection.

God is in the details.

LUDWIG MIES VAN DER ROHE

> ⚷ On the bar below, each of you write your initials to indicate how you define "intimacy."
>
> |—————————————+—————————————|
>
> Talking together   Doing things together
>
> Discuss what kinds of things you can do together that help create a sense of intimacy for the partner in your marriage who is more likely to feel closeness in that manner.

57

MAKE SURE YOUR SPOUSE IS DATED

To prevent our marriages from going sour or stale, we need to make sure our spouses are dated. I'm not referring here to purple stamps on cuts of beef or expiration dates on containers of milk. I'm talking about continuing to court one another by dating each other throughout your married life.

People in great marriages realize that romance and quality time are as important after the wedding as before. Thinking of dating as something one does until "hitched" and then allowing it to fade away because there is no longer a need to attract a mate is a good way to allow a marriage to sink into ordinariness or boredom—or worse.

One way to make sure your spouse is dated is simply to choose a regular date time and block it out in your calendars. If a consistent time doesn't work or doesn't fit your style, periodic communication about when to spend date time is necessary.

Dating need not require a lot of money. A bicycle ride, a walk, a rollerblade or stroll in a park can make a great date. Letting the kids sleep outside in a tent can make space for a great date in your own home. Be inventive! There's a lot more to do than dinner and a movie.

Dating works best if both partners take the initiative for organizing creative, fun, or romantic dates. Alternating who plans the dates requires communication but ensures that the initiative for dating is shared. We find that planning our dates as surprises adds an additional, delightful twist. When I know Claudia is planning a simple surprise for Saturday evening, I remember what it felt like as a kid waiting for Christmas. That kind of energy keeps marriage from feeling like a routine march of days.

Love just doesn't sit there, like a stone, it has to be made, like bread; re-made all the time, made new.

URSULA LE GUIN

The nemesis of a good marriage is monotony unrelieved by imagination.

JUDITH WALLERSTEIN
AND SANDRA BLAKESLEE

> ⚷ If you do not already have a regular date schedule (such as once per week), talk about how often you want to go on dates. Get out your calendars and put a hold on the times you choose. Discuss who will take the initiative for planning the dates and for getting a baby-sitter (if needed). Also talk about how much money you can afford to spend on such dates, and brainstorm some ideas for having a good time together.

CREATE A CULTURE OF AFFECTION

When he's outdoors, our golden retriever Bacchus is contained by an invisible fence system. The radio transmitter for the system displays a green light when the buried wire loop that forms the invisible fence is intact. When the wire is broken (by an errant shovel, for instance), the light goes out, telling us that the connection has been severed. When the wire is repaired, the light comes on again.

Touch functions this way in a close marriage. Physical affection exchanged several times per day between spouses sends the signal, "We are connected." When conflict disrupts the couple's emotional connection, their ability to touch is temporarily disrupted too. It is difficult to hug or touch someone affectionately when conflict is in the air. A couple who has not learned to make connection the norm in their marriage often allows several days or even weeks to go by while both partners simmer on the conflict and wonder how and when they might be able to be affectionate again. They avoid one another like Bacchus avoids that electric wire!

In a close marriage, the partners want to reestablish their connection as soon as possible after the initial upset has calmed down. They look for the opportunity to offer a hug, apologize, and discuss the conflict so that they can be connected again. (See "Reconnect after conflict," page 83, for more on this process.)

Touch is the first form of communication every human being experiences. Before we can talk or babble or coo, we know the language of touch. During the first months of our lives, we learn that being held tenderly helps when a case of diaper rash or abdominal gas is spoiling our day. Years later, when we feel hurt in some way in our married lives, touch retains its almost magical power to heal.

Touch is "sacramental," by which I mean that it has the power to be a tender and recurrent sign of God's presence in your marriage. Touch has the ability to express love, soothe sorrow, calm anxiety, de-escalate anger, and make working through conflict an experience that builds emotional intimacy rather than destroys it.

Talk not of wasted affection! Affection never was wasted . . .
HENRY WADSWORTH LONGFELLOW

You cannot do a kindness too soon because you never know how soon it will be too late.
RALPH WALDO EMERSON

In addition, touch just plain feels good! Helping each other feel good several times per day is great medicine for any marriage. Living together gives plenty of opportunities for rubbing each other the wrong way. It's important that we take the time to rub each other the right way—every day!

Every home has its own culture—the way things are done under that particular roof. Make your home a place where affection flows freely every day. This is crucial to establishing what your day-to-day experience of marriage will be. It also provides the best possible training ground for children to see what a close marriage looks like.

Agree early in your marriage—or at whatever point you are—to touch with affection daily. Then make it happen. Greet each other warmly when you have been apart, cuddle daily, offer spontaneous warm touches or rubs. It's difficult to do too much of this (unless you're in public and annoying everyone around you!). Most couples over time do far too little of it. If you're in a marriage in which one partner feels suffocated by the other's frequent affection, make clarifying the role of touch in your daily life part of visioning meetings. Get clear on what you want for affection in your marriage. Then make it happen.

Kindness gives birth to kindness.

SOPHOCLES

Love consists in this, that two solitudes protect and touch and greet each other.

RAINER MARIA RILKE

Every person's experience of touch prior to marriage is as unique as the family in which he or she grew up. When life gets stressful, people often revert to the well-rehearsed patterns of their pre-marriage lives. For many married people, that means letting go of being "in touch" on a daily basis. Discuss your original families' approaches to affection and clarify the role you want touch to play in your marriage.

> ⚷ For fun, write down in your notebooks how long you think the hug or kiss you give one another as a greeting should last. Compare your answers. Do you want a one-second kiss on the cheek or a thirty-second loving embrace? The difference between a one-second kiss and a 30-second hug is way more than 29 seconds! What kind of greeting would communicate, "You are precious; I am delighted to be in your presence again"?

DO AN OIL CHECK REGULARLY

I remember when my brother forgot to check the oil in his first car for a few years. He was busy with a new job and not used to thinking about car maintenance. One day the engine just seized up, no longer able to operate on the few drops of oil left. The engine was a complete loss.

Some couples get so busy that they forget to read the level of connection in their marriages. A simple way to do this is to ask your partner, "How are we doing—are we connected?" If answered honestly (such as, "We're great, it's just a busy day!" or, "I feel distant" or, "I'm still upset about the fight yesterday"), this simple question helps determine how much connection or lack of connection exists in the relationship on a given day. It allows the couple to do their own kind of OIL (Our Interconnected Love) check. Are we really living in an intimate, interconnected way, or are we allowing large blocks of time to pass without connection? Go ahead and ask.

When marriages go day after day or month after month without an OIL check, they can seize up too. Car owners should do an oil check about every 1500 miles. Married partners who have difficulty reading signs of connection or disconnection should consider an OIL check about every 1500 minutes. (There are 1440 minutes in a day.)

Thoughtfulness, the kindly regard for others, is the beginning of holiness.

MOTHER TERESA

Many of us make the mistake of building our spiritual lives around major crises and great opportunities … It would actually be better to concentrate less on the great but rare events and to be ready for and open to the constant little ones that are the stuff of everyday living.

FRANCIS DE SALES

> ⚷ Talk about a phrase that you can both use to check the level of connection between you. Discuss how often you feel one of you should do an OIL check on your marriage. Agree to be honest (in a respectful way) whenever your spouse asks you such a question.

Speak Your Spouse's Love Language

Gary Chapman's *The Five Love Languages* introduced a creative new way to think about staying connected in marriage. Reading his book together can be a helpful way for couples to explore how each partner most wants to experience love. Chapman's idea is that there are five basic ways, or languages, for expressing and receiving love. When we try to express love in one manner, but our partner's "primary love language" is different from our own, we can end up with frustration or miscommunication.

Kind words can be short and easy to speak, but their echoes are truly endless.

MOTHER TERESA

I consider Chapman's love languages idea so important that I'm including it here as one of the core ideas for *Make connection the norm.* Chapman's five love languages are:

- ◆ **Words of affirmation:** hearing compliments, gratitude, or encouragement for who you are or the things you have done.
- ◆ **Quality time:** spending time focused just on one another.
- ◆ **Receiving gifts:** being delighted by flowers, a card, a weekend away.
- ◆ **Acts of service:** doing things to make life more enjoyable or easier for your partner.
- ◆ **Physical touch:** sharing affectionate touch and sexuality.

If a man feels most loved, for instance, when his wife shares words of affirmation, but she mainly expresses love by acts of service, he is likely to feel frustrated. Likewise, she will feel annoyed if he gives her lots of affirmation but does not express his love by doing his share around the house.

Just as there are thousands of languages across the face of the globe, I think there are far more than five love languages. In discussing Chapman's book with Claudia, we agreed that several other love languages are important to us, including "nurturing dreams," "praying together" and "heart-to-heart conversation." You and your partner may speak one or more additional love languages not mentioned here.

As Chapman notes, a spouse can go the length of a marriage without realizing that he or she tends to *offer* love in the manner in which he or she likes to *receive* love. This sounds consistent with the golden rule (love your spouse as yourself), but what we really need, Chapman says, is to remember to *love your spouse as he or she most wants to be loved.* Forgetting this can lead to unnecessary frustration, hurt, anger, or distance in a marriage.

Offering love in the language in which our partner most wants to receive it is a deeply spiritual approach to loving because it involves being other-centered (*I wonder how he would like to be loved*) rather than self-centered (*What's wrong with her that she doesn't appreciate the way I express love?*).

I'd rather have roses on my table than diamonds on my neck.

EMMA GOLDMAN

8—➤ Read and discuss *The Five Love Languages* together, one chapter at time. Let your spouse know what your primary love language is and learn to speak your partner's language more consistently.

If you don't choose to read the book, review the five love languages in the text (page 62). In a notebook, each of you write them down in order from most important to least important. If you want, you can also give each a rating from 0 (no importance to me) to 10 (couldn't be more important to me). Then talk with one another about how you can more effectively give love in the way in which your partner most wants to receive it.

STAY HEART-TO-HEART

One of the first things to go when a couple allows the overly-busy culture to determine the structure and quality of their lives is a heart-to-heart connection between them. Remember when it seemed like you could stay up all night talking about anything and everything? That sense of sharing one's deeply held hopes, dreams, fears, and anxieties is common among couples early in the process of falling in love. In ordinary marriages, such heart-to-heart discussions are crowded out by too many things to do, an ever-present fatigue, or a sense of distance between partners.

Walt Whitman wrote, "I am vast, I contain multitudes," and the same is true of you and your spouse. Often, however, married people treat each other as completely-known entities and forego a continuing exploration of the inner world of the other person. Convincing yourself that you know your partner like the back of your hand is a formula for marital boredom. With the adventuresome attitude I'm suggesting, even the back of your hand contains unknown multitudes! After all, do you really know all the bones, tendons, blood vessels, nerves, and muscles in that hand and how they work together so well? (All right, so maybe you're a hand doctor, but the rest of you get my point!)

A good friend who phoned me periodically during a time of transition in both of our lives began each conversation with, "How's your heart?" Remembering to ask such a question of one's life partner is a big step toward creating a lasting heart-to-heart intimacy.

On the next several pages we'll explore two ways to keep heart-to-heart communication flowing in your marriage: using the high/low question and writing 20/20 letters.

THE HIGH/LOW QUESTION

Greater intimacy and connection can be as simple as changing, "How was your day?" to, "Tell me a joy from your day." By inquiring about the joys and stresses in a spouse's heart, we acknowledge that she or he is far more than someone to help with the dishes, hold down a job, pay bills, or run kids here and there. Instead, we communicate an interest in the full humanity of the one with whom we have chosen to travel through life.

During a session years ago with a struggling couple, the wife told me that the main problem in the marriage was that her husband had no feelings. She believed he was simply incapable of communicating from the heart. I noticed as the meeting progressed that she was doing all the talking. This happens frequently in marriages. If one spouse is underfunctioning (he doesn't say much), the other overfunctions (she talks almost nonstop to fill the silence). After respectfully requesting that she be quiet for a moment, I asked her husband to tell me about a great joy and a great heartache that he carried inside. He immediately welled up with tears and talked eloquently about the beautiful and painful aspects of his life. When I inquired of the couple if they ever simply asked one another to discuss a deep joy or sorrow, they said it hadn't occurred to them to do that.

The best and most beautiful things in the world cannot be seen or even touched. They must be felt with the heart.

HELEN KELLER

> ⚷ A simple way to move from surface to heart-to-heart discussion is to ask your partner to tell you about a high and a low experience from the day and how each made him or her feel inside. Regularly doing this can create a sense of honoring the inner life of your partner and can help you come to know each other on a deeper level. Try it with your partner today.

LOVE LETTERS FOR 20/20 MARITAL VISION

When you first began dating your partner, did you exchange letters, cards, or e-mails full of heartfelt words or feelings? Most couples have at least some experience of how wonderful it feels to be on the receiving end of a written expression of love.

Love doesn't make the world go 'round. Love is what makes the ride worthwhile.

FRANKLIN JONES

Writing is an unusually powerful tool for deepening connection in marriage. This is because writing allows us to look within ourselves and express whatever we choose without being distracted or sidetracked, as can happen in the course of ordinary conversation. I have coached couples to spend as little as five minutes writing a letter to one another during a counseling session. Often these couples report that the kinds of things they express in even brief letters are more heartfelt and intimate than anything they have communicated to one another in years!

Marriage Encounter, an organization that has helped thousands of couples create better marriages, uses a writing exercise called the 10/10. This involves sitting down with one's spouse, writing for ten minutes, and then sharing with each other for ten more minutes about what was written. I prefer to call the exercise 20/20, both because Claudia and I find that more time is needed for us to really enter into the exercise and because the 20/20 name picks up on the "20/20 vision" concept. Indeed, marriages that periodically invest 40 minutes (20 writing, 20 discussing) in such an exercise will be well on their way to creating a unified vision of the beautiful marriage they wish to create together.

Claudia and I call them "love letters" because we believe that writing and sharing them is a real act of love. Calling them "love letters" does not mean they need to be mushy, although that's certainly not off-limits. They are love letters because we take the time to communicate honestly, respectfully, and openly in a way that's intended to benefit our marriage.

Some couples attempt to write the letters in journals separately and then meet together later to discuss what they have written. I have seen this approach become problematic. This is because one person often writes a great deal, whereas the other writes little or nothing before the meeting. What is intended to be a unifying exercise to increase intimacy can end up in a fight ("What do you mean you forgot to write?! I've got twelve pages here!") Therefore, I strongly recommend that you simply sit down together and take twenty minutes of quiet time to write before talking.

An important aspect of the 20/20 exercise is reading the letters out loud to one another. This is more effective than simply reading your partner's letter silently to yourself. Some people are self-conscious about their writing ability. Reading your own letter out loud means that your partner need not see your less-than-perfect spelling, grammar, or penmanship. Furthermore, reading a heartfelt letter that you have written allows whatever emotion is present in the letter to be expressed in your voice. The words on the paper are far more than words. They represent your joys and struggles. When you hear your partner read her or his letter to you out loud, this will connect with you at a deeper level than if he or she simply allowed you to read it silently to yourself.

It's important when writing the letters to follow a "sandwich" format. This means that the letter begins with affirmation of one's partner, proceeds to an inventory of one's heart (positive or difficult emotions), and ends with affirmation of one's partner. No one likes to receive a letter that begins with something like: "Dear Kevin, I'm so angry at you I could spit nails!" Remember, sandwiching the letter in affirmation of the essential goodness of your partner is crucial to making the 20/20 experience one that will increase intimacy rather than lead to conflict.

> *Relationships are meant to be a sign of God's love for humanity as a whole and each person in particular.*
>
> HENRI NOUWEN

THE SANDWICH FORMAT FOR 20/20 LETTERS

Dear _____,

- ◆ Affirm
- ◆ Write from the heart
- ◆ Affirm

Love,

_____

67

The 20/20 exercise is a tool that, when used regularly, has the potential to take your marriage to a level of intimacy that will surprise and delight you. Some people though, particularly many men, resist the idea of writing letters to enhance connection.

I remember a man at one of my workshops coming up to me and asking, "Do we really have to write these love letters?" After noticing his rough hands, I asked him if he was into woodworking. He said yes, and I asked him how many different saws he had in his wood shop. He told me about his hand saw, band saw, table saw, chop saw, hack saw, compound miter saw, and so on. I told him that every idea in this book is like one of those saws—a great tool to have to get a particular job done, and the only tool that can get certain jobs done.

It is only with the heart that one can see rightly; what is essential is invisible to the eye.

ANTOINE DE SAINT-EXUPERY

I invite spouses, male or female, who are reluctant to try 20/20 letters to realize that "playing the game of marriage" at the highest level requires a number of intimacy skills, just as surely as being a competent woodworker requires familiarity with many tools. Set aside forty minutes sometime soon and discover the closeness that this exercise can create.

Sharing common interests, dating, being affectionate daily, doing a periodic OIL check, speaking your partner's love language, using the high/low question or 20/20 letters for staying heart-to-heart—the more ways you intentionally make connection the norm of your relationship, the more you will experience marriage at its best. *Make connection the norm* is a spiritual practice because it is a daily commitment to showing basic love and consideration—thereby keeping the marriage close and strong.

SAMPLE 20/20 LETTER

Dear Joe,

[Affirmation]

I'm grateful that we are taking time to write and talk this morning. Thanks for everything in the past week—your contribution to the family financially, your being home for dinner, watching the kids on Wednesday when I was out with friends. I'm fortunate to have you as my life partner.

[Write from the heart]

I'm glad that spring is here. It's been wonderful to get out for some gardening and to begin exercising outdoors again. I'm looking forward to our weekend away in May—let's talk some more about planning for that getaway.

Work has been really stressful lately. I know the money and benefits are good, but I find myself wondering if this is what I want to do with my life. I'd like to talk with you about how we would be financially if I decided to go back to school and eventually switch jobs.

It's not been the best week for us. Monday was pretty tense—do we need to talk more about the angry words we had? I still feel like our affection is a little off since then. I miss your hugs. Let's make love tonight—the week's been too busy and we've been disconnected—we need some good lovin'. I know you want me to initiate more—it's difficult when we've not been that connected this week, but I'm ready to get past that.

[Affirmation]

Know that I love you deeply, Joe. Thanks for listening. I'm fortunate to have a man like you for a husband. Thanks for being my lover and friend.

Love always,

Tricia

To Have and to Laugh

Slight Miscommunication

Wife: "Honey, I'll be going to lunch today with my old boyfriend Norm like you suggested."

Husband: "I said, 'You need to make connection the norm,' not 'You need to make a connection with Norm!'"

Some people ask the secret of our long marriage. We take time to go to a restaurant two times a week. A little candlelight, dinner, soft music and dancing. She goes Tuesdays, I go Fridays.

HENNY YOUNGMAN

Key Summary Points
MAKE CONNECTION THE NORM

- Expect to feel connected or "on track" with one another every day. When you do not, do what is necessary to heal what has come between you (see next chapter).
- Some people think of intimacy as doing things together. Discuss how you can each share some of the other's life interests.
- Clarify how often you will go on dates together and hold time for them in your calendars. Share initiative for planning dates.
- Clarify how often and in what ways you wish to be affectionate with one another on a daily basis. Create a culture of affection in your home.

◆ Do an OIL (Our Interconnected Love) check periodically by simply asking your partner, "How are we doing—are we connected?"

◆ Learn to give love the way your partner most enjoys receiving love. Read *The Five Love Languages* for more on this idea.

◆ Agree that your marriage will be one that maintains a deep heart-to-heart connection.

◆ Ask, "What was a high or low from your day?" instead of "How was your day?" to create deeper emotional connection.

◆ Take quiet time periodically to write 20/20 love letters; then read and discuss them.

DISCUSSION QUESTIONS

1. Daily affection is a basic way to make connection the norm. Do you give and receive affection freely in your relationship with your partner, or is this an area in which you can grow?

2. Chapman's five love languages are listed on page 62. What is your primary love language? What do you think your partner's primary love language is? How can each of you learn to speak your partner's love language more effectively?

3. The chapter presented two ways to keep connected heart-to-heart with your partner: the high/low question (page 64) and the 20/20 love letter (pages 65-69). Why do you think some couples lose a deeper form of communication? Which of the two methods of staying heart-to-heart do you think fits your relationship best?

4. How often do you currently go on dates with one another? Are you both satisfied with that arrangement? Do you like the idea of alternating who plans the dates? Do you think having the dates serve as little surprises in your life would be helpful to break up your normal routine?

Notice how the checker-like design representing a calendar in Make connection the norm *is carried over into the depiction above (see cover or page 14). This represents how our efforts at daily connection flow directly into our attempts to bring honoring to conflict. The faint upside-down head is listening to an open heart, through which can be seen the whole universe—a portrayal of the power of empathic listening. The bullseye-like circles represent two people connected at their centers (heart to heart) by making conflict a path to intimacy.*

3

BRING HONORING TO CONFLICT

SUMMARY OF THIS PRACTICE

Many couples have great difficulty returning to a close connection after conflict. Their efforts to make connection the norm can be easily derailed by the rub that comes with sharing life with another person. *Bring honoring to conflict* means letting your closeness be stronger than your conflict. It means hugging, apologizing, and talking soon after tension has subsided instead of distancing, waiting for your partner's apology, or going silent. It is crucial to maintaining the daily loving connection that is at the core of a Namaste marriage.

The "winner" of a marital fight is the first one to offer a hug, apologize, and suggest talking it over in a more honoring way.

SPIRITUAL FOCUS
FOR THIS PRACTICE

*Love is patient, love is kind . . . it is not rude,
it does not seek its own interests . . . it is not quick-
tempered, it does not brood over injury.*

1 Corinthians 13: 4-6

*A*ll married people experience conflict and sometimes fall short of the ideal in handling their tensions. This may seem obvious, but some couples privately fear that others have found the secret to living happily ever after without any conflict. Seeing your own marriage from the inside is different from seeing others' marriages from the outside. No one does this thing called marriage perfectly, so we all need to learn to deal with conflict.

When approached in an honoring way, conflict is not just a necessary evil in marriage; rather, it is an essential component of the path to intimacy and to spiritual growth. Learning to handle conflict is as crucial to a marriage's health as kidneys are to the body's health. Without a way to eliminate small, daily toxins, many marriages do not make it, and some of those that do survive do not learn to thrive.

Bring honoring to conflict means that you allow your enduring honoring energy to be stronger than your momentary upset energy. This requires that during a conflict you avoid foul, threatening, contemptuous, or abusive language and behavior (see Appendix B, p. 208). It also means that when you've calmed down after a conflict, you hug and express your love for one another before talking about the problem and maintain a loving physical connection and voice tone as you review the conflict.

If you've ever seen a horse around an electric fence wire, you know how they are simply terrified of that thin line! For some people, being asked to engage conflict directly is like asking a horse to brush against an electric wire that has given it too many jolts in the past. Some people find conflict frightening because they were raised in a chronically conflicted home or because conflict has caused too much "jolting" in their own marriage. These people know that conflict should be dealt with as it arises, but lacking the skills to do so, they typically get caught in a cycle of ignoring it, letting it build up, and then blowing up. This cycle can take thirty minutes or thirty years, but it always results from an inability to engage conflict in an honoring way.

The appealing notion that a good marriage is conflict-free and that good communication can avoid anger have gained popularity. But every married person knows that "conflict-free marriage" is an oxymoron. In reality it is neither possible nor desirable.

JUDITH WALLERSTEIN
AND SANDRA BLAKESLEE

Life is difficult. This is a great truth, one of the greatest truths. It is a great truth because once we truly see this truth, we transcend it.

M. SCOTT PECK

Other couples try to live as if conflict is not a part of married life. They are intent on keeping up the facade of perfection, as if to convince themselves that there is not a single fault line in their relationship. This avoidant approach can develop from having experienced too much conflict in early life or having been raised in a home in which conflict was avoided at all costs.

Bring honoring to conflict is the practice that couples rate as most important for them to learn about in my workshops. This chapter contains what you need to know about approaching conflict in an honoring way. These conflict resolution ideas, however, require practice—lots of it! Claudia and I have been working on them for twenty years, and we both still have much to learn about honoring, especially when life turns up the heat. So consider the need to learn about *Bring honoring to conflict* a continuous process on the marriage journey.

Note: Several ideas in this chapter are influenced by marriage expert John Gottman's work. These include the three styles of conflict, solving solvable problems, recurrent conflicts, and looking for the dream behind the conflict. Readers interested in learning more about Gottman's work can consult his seminal work, *The Marriage Clinic*, or his several slimmer books for lay readers.

Sooner or later, in response to the problems of daily living, individual will reasserts itself. He wants to have sex; she doesn't . . . He wants to put money in the bank; she wants a dishwasher . . . At this point they begin either to dissolve the ties of their relationship or initiate the work of real loving.

M. Scott Peck

Nested Meditation

I picked you.

I picked you
to be my wife.

I picked you
to be my wife
and I didn't know you.

I picked you
to be my wife
and I didn't know you
were a wildflower.

For whatever reason, recently or years ago, you picked each other to go through life together. You thought you knew everything about each other, but the years revealed (or will reveal) how much you didn't know. Learning to discuss conflicts in an honoring way allows beauty to blossom from what you thought was only brokenness.

┌───┐
│   **PRACTICING**   │
│   *BRING HONORING TO CONFLICT*   │
│   **IN YOUR MARRIAGE**   │
└───┘

THE SEVEN-STEP MODEL OF CONFLICT RESOLUTION

Most couples don't have an explicit model for dealing with conflict. They just make it up as they go. Below is a model that, if you learn and use it, will transform your ability to deal with conflict.

Step 1:   Have the conflict (the easiest step, except for conflict-avoidant types).

Step 2:   Use time-outs to stop destructive interactions.

Step 3:   Reconnect after conflict.

Step 4:   Exchange mutual, no-fault apologies.

Step 5:   Use empathic listening to review the conflict.

Step 6:   Solve solvable problems.

Step 7:   Enjoy being close and connected again.

Some people, when first seeing the seven steps, feel overwhelmed. *You have to be kidding,* they think. *You expect me to do all that every time there's a conflict in our marriage?!* Consider swinging a golf club: a pro makes it look easy, but it actually consists of many steps (determine distance to the hole, select club, take practice swings, stand over ball, execute backswing, make

> *The best way out is always through.*
>
> ROBERT FROST

It usually takes two people to make one of them angry.
LAURENCE PETER

contact, follow through—and, in my case, go search for the ball in the woods!). When practiced throughout the course of your marriage, the seven steps of conflict resolution will flow naturally from one to the other, just as the steps of hitting a golf ball become second nature.

THE SEVEN-STEP MODEL: SUSAN AND MARK

Here is an overview to give you a sense of how the seven-step model works. A couple I worked with in marriage counseling, let's call them Susan and Mark, told me of a conflict over his coming home late from work one evening without calling her to tell her he'd be late. Step 1, Have the conflict, can be summarized as follows:

- ◆ Mark didn't call to say he was delayed.
- ◆ He came home ninety minutes late.
- ◆ Susan vented her upset with him as soon as he came in the door.
- ◆ Mark said he thought he'd told her he had a late meeting that day.
- ◆ Susan said, "You never communicate enough with me about these things!"
- ◆ Both of their voices had begun to get too loud, and some unkind statements had begun to bounce between them.

Step 2 (Use time-outs to stop destructive interactions) occurred when Susan said, "I'm really feeling upset about this. I need a time-out right now. Can we talk about it when the kids are asleep?" Later, after they had tucked their children into bed, Mark approached Susan with open arms and said, "I'd like to talk about it with you so we can feel close again." Susan welcomed his hug and completed step 3 (Reconnect after conflict). As they continued embracing, Susan said, "I'm sorry about the tension we had—I want to be close to you again too." Mark reciprocated the apology. They had successfully completed step 4 (Exchange mutual, no-fault apologies) and avoided the trap of spending the next day or several days feeling distant from one another.

After hugging, they spent a full hour in step 5 (Use empathic listening to review the conflict), making sure to use "I language," watch nonverbals, and listen deeply to one another (see pages 87-95). Mark learned that Susan was quite worried about him when he was late coming home, wondering if he'd had an accident. Her anger had been, in its own way, an expression of her love for him and her fear of losing him. He also learned that she treasures their mealtimes together with the children and became upset when work takes precedence over their marriage and family, which had been happening more frequently of late.

Susan learned that Mark was feeling much more pressured at work since several colleagues had been laid off, leaving him with more work to do and a sense that he'd better go the extra mile or face eventually being laid off himself. She learned that he was more deeply dissatisfied with his work than she had been aware. The conflict over his being late from work led to a heartfelt discussion about balance between work and family and how to create the kind of marriage they wanted together.

Step 6 (Solve solvable problems) went quickly. Mark admitted the need to stand up more firmly at work for family time and to avoid scheduling meetings that would run late. He also agreed to let Susan know if a late meeting was unavoidable.

They glowed in my office as they described how they had experienced the heart-to-heart intimacy and honesty of working through the conflict. Avoiding time lost to cold-shouldering and actually using conflict to build intimacy rather than destroy it felt like a major breakthrough for them.

In this instance, Mark and Susan took a full hour to listen deeply to one another. Engaging conflict in a manner that has the potential to build intimacy requires far more time than band-aid approaches intended to just get past the incident as quickly as possible.

Almost all married people fight, although many are ashamed to admit it. Actually a marriage in which no quarreling at all takes place may well be the one that is dead or dying from emotional undernourishment. If you care, you probably fight.

FLORA DAVIS

STEP 1: HAVE THE CONFLICT

Each of us grows up witnessing how our parents or parent figures dealt with conflict. Over time, these patterns soak into us and form our own approaches to conflict. Relationship experts have a variety of ways of describing common approaches to dealing with conflict in marriage. John Gottman, the researcher who has contributed greatly to our understanding of conflict in marriage, separates people into three categories:

Volatile: Likely to get angry quickly and to want to get issues "on the table," often with blunt honesty.

Validating: Slower to anger, wanting to discuss issues in a calmer manner and attempting to understand a partner's views and feelings.

Avoiding: Uncomfortable with any kind of conflict; deals with conflict by avoiding it.

I call these the "three V's of conflict" (because each starts with or contains a "v"). Most marriage counselors teach spouses to approach conflict in a validating way. Gottman's research, however, indicates that it is the mismatch of styles (especially a volatile person married to an avoiding person) that creates the biggest problems. Two volatile people can do fairly well together as long as they avoid abusive interactions. Two avoiding people often live quite peacefully together, though clinical experience indicates that these are often the couples who present for therapy in a crisis saying, "We never had a problem for thirty years, and now we're on the verge of divorce!" According to Gottman, then, not every stable marriage has two validating people in it. I teach, however, that volatile and avoiding spouses do best when each tries to move to the middle ground (validating) when they are reviewing a conflict.

Each partner's approach to conflict is usually a strong "habit energy" that does not change easily. There is a difference, though,

You can accomplish by kindness what you cannot by force.

PUBLILIUS SYRUS

between our approach to having a conflict and the approach we use to revisit, discuss, and heal a conflict, which should be near the golden mean of "validating." Over time, learning to heal conflicts with honoring can help a volatile spouse become less volatile and an avoidant spouse become less avoidant.

⌐⊶ Discuss the following questions regarding your mother, father, or other significant caregiving figures:

1. Which of the three approaches to conflict did each tend toward?
2. What approach to conflict did you develop over time by exposure to what you saw in your childhood home?
3. As a couple, are your approaches to conflict similar or different?
4. How can each of you move toward the middle ground of "validating"?

STEP 2: USE TIME-OUTS TO STOP DESTRUCTIVE INTERACTIONS

We all know we should keep a fire extinguisher in our homes so it will be available in an emergency. Few couples, however, have a mutually-agreed-upon plan for putting out marital fires. In fact, some married people behave as if the best way to respond when a conflict ignites is to throw gasoline on the blaze! This belief that "getting the anger out" is always healthy can be traced, in part, to the fact that many relationship experts used to encourage a full venting of anger.

We know now from Gottman's research that once physiological arousal has escalated beyond a certain point, nothing good is likely to happen in an interaction. His studies suggest that this point of no return is around 95-100 heartbeats per minute. The

Our peace will be found in the midst of warfare, our serenity will be bought at the price of surrender.

FRANCIS DE SALES

best strategy, if the discussion appears to be headed for a hurtful fight, is to stop and take a break from one another. This is called "taking a time-out." The function of this practice is to put out marital fires before one or both of you get burned.

When it comes to time-outs, the "no questions asked" rule applies. When one partner says, "I want a time-out," the other grants the request without question or delay. After a brief determination of when you will reconvene in a calmer manner, the overheated interaction is simply ended. No final words or parting shots, no slamming doors or stomping out of the room—just an agreement to take a break and try later to create a more honoring interaction.

To use the time-out effectively, it is important to actually agree on the specific words that will be used (or gestures, such as a "T" made with the hands to signal "time-out"). Phrases such as, "Could we talk about this later?" or, "I don't want to deal with this right now" may not be perceived as requests for a time-out. Agree ahead of time that the words "time-out" will be the cue to stop the interaction, or select other words that suit you. Then make sure those exact words are used when making the request.

There are several reasons that some couples are reluctant to use a time-out. First, some people still believe that "getting all the anger out on the table" is best. That approach is only helpful if both of you remain honoring, a hard trick to pull off when the emotions of anger or hurt are escalating. Second, some people don't want to grant their partners the power, by using the words "time-out," to stop a conflict. Third, some are concerned that if a time-out is granted, the more avoidant partner will attempt to drop or escape the conflict altogether by forgetting it or resisting later attempts to discuss it in a calmer way. This pattern of avoidance after a time-out is common among those who do not like even a whiff of conflict in the air. Such people believe that it is not possible to discuss difficult material in a calm and honoring way. Finally, if a person overuses time-outs, perhaps asking for them as soon as a discussion becomes uncomfortable, the part-

Speak when you're angry and you'll make the best speech you'll ever regret.

HENRY WARD BEECHER

Often the difference between a successful marriage and a mediocre one consists of leaving about three or four things a day unsaid.

HARLAN MILLER

ner may feel time-outs are not helpful. If you use a time-out too much without good reason, your partner may begin to feel you're just dodging conflict. On the other hand, if your partner is using time-outs frequently, it's a good opportunity to reflect on your own volatility—and your capacity to create strong negative emotion in your partner by the way you handle conflict.

The time-out is a basic, effective practice that should, like a fire extinguisher, be in every couple's home. Yet most couples do not have this safeguard ready for use in their home. Make sure it's in yours.

> Talk briefly about what kind of phrase or signal you will use when you need a time-out. Agree that when one person asks for a time-out, the other will grant it immediately and that you will reconvene when calm to discuss the situation. Practice actually saying the words to each other in preparation for when you need them in a real conflict.

STEP 3: RECONNECT AFTER CONFLICT

Imagine that you have made it to fifty or more years of marriage and that one of you is near death. As you prepare to say goodbye, both of you realize that you spent nearly two thousand of the twenty thousand days of your marriage in silent distance after conflict.

Queen Elizabeth I in the early 17th century is reported to have uttered as her last words, "All my possessions for a moment of time!" I wonder how many couples might feel something like that as they look back at so many days of happiness lost because they didn't know how to reconnect after conflict.

You cannot shake hands with a clenched fist.

INDIRA GANDHI

Forgiveness is not an occasional act; it is a permanent attitude.

MARTIN LUTHER KING, JR.

We must make our homes centers of compassion and forgive endlessly.

MOTHER TERESA

Reconnecting is easy to explain, but a bit harder to do. The idea is straightforward. As soon as both partners are reasonably calm after a conflict, look for an opportunity to offer a hug. Physically reconnecting in this way conveys a clear message: "You are still my beloved, and this conflict has not changed that." Offering a hug after a conflict is using the daily connection that you have built into your marriage to help get you back on track. This is what we mean by *Bring honoring to conflict.*

Most people instinctively want to wait to touch affectionately again until *after* the conflict has been resolved. I teach couples the opposite: Use the strength of your daily affectionate connection to re-establish a sense of connection so that you can re-engage in an honoring way the issue that created the tension. This is how conflict is transformed from a frightening aspect of marriage to an opportunity to learn and grow together. Bringing your affection to the effort to "mend fences" after conflict creates a safe haven that allows honoring to be present as you work through the source of the conflict.

The physical reconnection that occurs with a hug can be extended into a calmer discussion of the issue that created the conflict. This is achieved by holding hands or sitting so that there is some physical contact while you talk about what caused the tension. Touch communicates soothing and honoring. It is less likely that the second attempt at discussing the issue will flare up if you remain in affectionate connection as you talk.

The reason so many days are lost to cold silence in lots of marriages is that people simply don't know how to re-establish affectionate touch. The solution is simple: Just do it.

I remember the first time I was fitted with rappelling gear and instructed to walk off the edge of a cliff. Everything in me was saying it was unnatural and dangerous, but when I did it, the experience was beautiful and freeing. You will feel the same way when you learn to reconnect after conflict.

> ⚷ Give each other permission to offer a hug after a conflict has settled down. Agree to hug *before* talking about the problem again. Agree that you will not reject a hug when it is offered as a symbol of reconnection. Make sure you start your discussion of the problem with an affectionate symbol of your honoring for each other (such as holding hands while you talk). Don't re-engage a conflict with the same negative energy you had before.

STEP 4:
EXCHANGE MUTUAL, NO-FAULT APOLOGIES

As much as some married people struggle with reconnecting after conflict, many have even more difficulty with apologizing. Countless "cold, silent" days are caused by both partners waiting for the other to apologize first. Everyone knows how that thinking goes: *I'm not apologizing. It was their fault. Let them apologize.* This is a recipe for cold marriage stew.

There is a way out of the "I'm not apologizing" standoff. I call it "mutual, no-fault apologies." This sounds something like an insurance policy, and that's what it provides for your marriage. It insures you against lost time and further hurt feelings.

A no-fault apology goes something like this:

> *"I'm sorry we had that conflict. I don't like feeling tense with you. You are special to me, and I'd like to make another try at talking about it."*

Notice that in this apology, there is no attempt to determine who was to blame; therefore, it is a "no-fault" apology. Certainly we can all think of times when an "I-was-to-blame" apology is called for, but this is not the majority of cases in marriage. Conflicts are usually over relatively small things. Normally both parties participate in creating or escalating the tension—or in avoiding a productive discussion about it. Small conflicts become bigger conflicts when fanned by the flames of defensiveness, accumulated

Be the first to forgive, to smile and take the first step, and you will see happiness bloom ...

ROBERT MULLER

When a deep injury is done to us, we can never recover until we forgive ...

ALAN PATON

85

The weak can never forgive. Forgiveness is an attribute of the strong.

Mohandas Gandhi

unresolved tensions, or the reality that seemingly trivial behaviors can be symbolic of larger issues in the relationship. Empathic listening (see page 87) is often successful at helping determine why something small caused big hurt between you.

We've covered the "no fault" part of this approach to apologizing, but what about the "mutual" part? These apologies are mutual because both spouses apologize. Whoever says first, "I'm sorry we had that tension" can expect to hear similar words from her or his partner. In general, demanding that your partner take blame or offer a more prolonged apology (on his or her knees perhaps!) will not move you toward the kind of honoring interaction that occurs in empathic listening. Obviously, truly serious hurts, such as abuse or infidelity, require more than a quick apology. In fact, insincere apologies in such cases can perpetuate a cycle of hurt, making things look healed for a time when nothing has really changed. Forgiveness in these cases, if it occurs, is usually a process that takes considerable time. The vast majority of smaller marital conflicts, however, are put most effectively on the path of healing when mutual, no-fault apologies are exchanged.

The practice of reconnection and mutual apologies in marriage is a built-in way of making forgiveness a part of your relationship. A good marriage, it is said, is made of two givers and two forgivers. I think Jesus' admonition to forgive seventy times seven times actually comes up a bit short for married couples. Given the reality that we can forgive a spouse for something nearly every day, seventy times seven times (490) only gets us through the first year or two!

> ⚷ The next time you have a small conflict, wait until the dust has settled a bit. Then approach your spouse with a warm hug and say, "I'm sorry we had that tension. I'd like to talk about it calmly with you." Again, be sure to maintain some affectionate touch while you talk to minimize the chance that the conflict will flare up again.

STEP 5: USE EMPATHIC LISTENING TO REVIEW THE CONFLICT

The "Love is patient, love is kind" passage from St. Paul, on which the spiritual practice of *Bring honoring to conflict* is based, is the most frequently-used reading at Christian weddings. Nowhere is Paul's vision of love more important than in our efforts to listen deeply to our partners following an episode of conflict. When we offer genuine listening to our partners, we love in a form close to what Paul envisioned.

After a conflict has occurred, a time-out has been taken (if needed), and reconnection and mutual apologies have occurred, it is important to spend time exploring the conflict in a calmer manner. At the heart of this fifth step of conflict resolution is what I call "empathic listening." Counselors also call it "active listening" or "deep listening." Empathy is *feeling with* another person, seeing the world from behind another's eyes, walking a mile in his or her moccasins.

Empathic listening involves a sort of backwards approach to listening. Most people in a conflict try to impose their feelings or point of view on the other person. When two people attempt to do this at once, a discussion quickly begins to feel like it's going nowhere, or worse, like it's a runaway train heading straight for a marital pileup. Empathic listening means putting aside your agenda, opinions, and feelings so that you can listen intently to the other person.

In *Fighting for Your Marriage,* Howard Markman and his colleagues have coined a clever phrase for this kind of listening: "Pass the floor." They give spouses a small piece of vinyl flooring (or more recently, a checkered piece of paper that symbolizes tile flooring) to pass between them as a symbol for "who has the floor." The spouse with the floor uses "I statements" to talk about feelings, the other spouse focuses on empathic listening. The floor is passed back and forth to make it clear who is taking the speaking role and who is focusing on empathic listening.

Honoring your spouse enough to suspend your own feelings to listen deeply is a great gift to your marriage. When you make

I shall become a master in this art only after a great deal of practice.

ERICH FROMM

87

space for your spouse to really speak from the heart about a conflict, it's amazing what you can learn.

Pages 88 to 95 will teach you more about how to do empathic listening well. For an extended written example of empathic listening, see Appendix C, page 217.

Empathic Listening
STAYING IN ROLE

The box on page 90 contains important guidelines for empathic listening. They are explained in more detail as the chapter proceeds.

The first step in empathic listening is determining speaker and listener. These are clearly-defined roles as described on page 90. Empathic listening does not follow the "back and forth" pattern of ordinary conversation, in which partners take turns trying to convince each other of the rightness of their positions. In empathic listening, we stay in role (either speaker or listener) for as long as necessary to allow deep listening to occur. Switch roles only when the speaker is able to say, "OK, thanks for listening to me; I'd like to listen to you now."

Staying in role is perhaps the most challenging part of empathic listening. The listener needs to put aside any and all opinions, judgments, reactions, comebacks, or objections that will get in the way of offering the gift of pure listening. This is indeed a practice of love!

One helpful hint is to realize that the words LISTEN and SILENT have the same six letters. While the listener role involves more than being silent, most of the time the listener is silent, simply giving space and brief verbal encouragements ("Uh-huh...") which convey the message, "I am listening." Remember: In the listening role, less is more. Say enough to convey you are listening to the speaker's feelings, but do not go on and on and derail the empathic listening process.

There is no such thing as conversation. It is an illusion. There are intersecting monologues, that is all.
REBECCA WEST

You will know when you are trying too hard . . . There will be an increase in talking and a decrease in listening.
WILLIAM MARTIN

> ⚷ Practice the idea of staying in role by asking each other to talk about three of your favorite things in life and why you like them. After your partner tells you each of the three, repeat it back in your own words to indicate you were listening. Don't say, "Yes, I like that too," or "I can't stand that!" Just practice staying in role—one of you talking, the other listening. Then switch roles. In addition to staying in role, this exercise demonstrates how empathic listening can be used to discuss any aspect of your life together, not just conflict.

Empathic Listening
USING "I LANGUAGE"

The quickest way to make your partner defensive when you are in the speaking role is to use lots of "you language." Consider the difference between the following two approaches to a rather typical conflict over household duties:

The first duty of love is to listen.

PAUL TILLICH

Ineffective: "You never help with the laundry; you're always coming in asking, 'Is dinner ready yet?' You haven't cleaned a toilet in years! You're just not pulling your weight around here!"

More effective: "I'm feeling overwhelmed by everything there is to get done around here—laundry, cooking, cleaning. I would like it if you could give me some help. I'd like to talk with you about a plan to address this."

GUIDELINES FOR EMPATHIC LISTENING

BOTH PARTNERS:

Determine who is the speaker and who is the listener. Stay in these roles until the speaker is able to say, "I feel heard. I want to listen to you now." Do not jump out of role! Talk about problems when you can focus without interruptions. Turn the television off, don't answer the phone, and make sure that children are occupied or in bed.

SPEAKER:

1. Use "I language" (see p. 89). Avoid accusatory "you language." A helpful formula for some people is: "When _____ happens, I feel _____, because _____."
2. Keep your voice tone, eye contact, gestures, and other nonverbal communications calm and honoring (see page 94-95).
3. Allow breaks in your own turn at speaking so that your partner can offer reflections.

LISTENER:

1. Put your own opinions and feelings aside while listening (easy to say, much harder to do!).
2. Engage your partner with good nonverbals (gestures, eye contact, and so on—see pages 94-95).
3. Give signs that you are actively tracking what your partner is saying (nodding your head, saying "Uh-huh"—any indicator that you are not allowing your attention to wander to your own thoughts or reactions).
4. Use "reflections" (repeat in your own words what you have heard your partner say—see page 92-93).
5. Encourage your partner to say more or go deeper by using simple phrases like, "Say more about that," or "Help me understand that better."
6. Don't just reflect the content of what your partner is saying; reflect the *feelings* that are being expressed. Listen carefully for feeling words (such as frustrated, hurt, disappointed, afraid, or sad), and let your partner know that you are hearing and trying to understand her or his feelings.

Notice how the ineffective example included five *you, you're,* and *your* statements. I've coded couple interactions in counseling sessions and found that some people use forty or more *you* or *your* phrases in a five-minute time period. There are few people who can avoid getting defensive when barraged with *you* and *your.* The more effective statement on page 89 shows how "I language" is much less likely to provoke defensiveness.

Beyond "you language," other dangerous words include *always* and *never.* Any time we hear those words, our natural inclination is to look for exceptions ("What do you mean *never?* Just last week . . ."). Looking for exceptions prevents us from listening to our partners.

In really trying to practice using "I language," be sure to make a genuine attempt at focusing on your feelings instead of attacking your partner in some way. Saying, "I feel you are really woefully irresponsible" is not really "I language." It is camouflaged "you language."

Using lots of "you's" in your language is guaranteed to produce results: an angry, defensive spouse who is rendered incapable of listening to what you are trying to say. Make an agreement with each other that if one of you begins using lots of "you language," the other will simply and calmly say, "I'll listen better if you use 'I language.'"

The principal form that the work of love takes is attention. When we love another we give him or her our attention; we attend to that person's growth . . . By far the most common and important way in which we can exercise our attention is by listening. We spend an enormous amount of time listening, most of which we waste, because on the whole most of us listen very poorly.

M. Scott Peck

If you want to study this aspect of your marital interaction in more depth, try tape-recording a fifteen-minute discussion between the two of you about a conflicted issue. Then listen to it and write down all the "you" statements. Think about how they could be turned into "I language."

The heart has its reasons which reason does not understand.

BLAISE PASCAL

Empathic Listening
USING REFLECTIONS

When you order at the drive-through of a fast food restaurant, the worker always repeats your order to make sure she or he heard it right: "You ordered a burger, fries, and a cola. Is that correct?" This is part of what the listener does in empathic listening. By rephrasing in his or her own words what the other person has said and asking if it has been heard accurately, the listener conveys a willingness to stay focused on the speaker (instead of rebutting, disagreeing, fighting, giving an opinion, or other unhelpful responses).

When you are the listener, keep using these reflective statements (or "reflections") until your spouse says, "OK, I think you've heard me. We can switch to listening to you now." It bears repeating: Don't switch roles casually. Stay in your roles of speaker and listener until you agree to switch.

> Practice offering each other a reflection in the following way. Take turns speaking about the details of your day for one full minute. After one minute, allow your partner to repeat what you said in his or her own words. This will sound something like, "OK, what you just said was . . ." Do not add anything to what your partner said. Just paraphrase it in your own words. By doing this, you convey that your attention was focused on listening.

Empathic Listening
REFLECTING FEELINGS AND "TELL ME MORE"

Try not to sound like a machine when you offer a reflection during empathic listening. The idea is to 1) demonstrate that you indeed were listening, and 2) reflect the feelings expressed by your partner in a way that indicates you are trying to understand them. There's a large difference between, "You told me your feelings about money" and "So you're feeling anxious whenever money comes up between us, kind of like anticipating that we'll have a fight, and you don't like all the tension it creates—is that what you're feeling?" The first sounds like a disinterested tape-recorder, the latter like a partner expressing concern and the desire to understand. It's not the number of words used by the listener in giving a reflection that's important. Rather, it is conveying that you are truly listening and trying to understand your partner's world that is the core of this approach. In general, though, don't give long, elaborate reflections that go beyond what your partner said. Simply convey that you have been listening deeply, then shift the focus back to your spouse.

Much—even most— meaning in conversation does not reside in the words spoken at all, but is filled in by the person listening.

DEBORAH TANNEN

When you have finished a reflection, end with a statement that encourages your partner to share more. A simple, "Tell me more about that" is often all that is needed. Again, do not switch roles by offering your reactions; just invite your partner to go deeper or further into whatever he or she wants to say.

As a way of practicing looking for the feeling in a partner's communication, tell each other about a difficult memory from high school or junior high school. As the speaker, talk about all the feelings you had at the time. As the listener, make a note of (or write down) every feeling word you hear. When you offer the reflection of what you heard, focus on the feelings. This will sound something like, "You said you felt really embarrassed, angry, betrayed, and suspicious of the person who hurt you for a long time. Does that cover it?" You don't need to reflect all the details of what your partner said. Reflecting the feelings is most important. That's why we call it empathic listening.

Empathic Listening

NONVERBAL COMMUNICATION

A man who rolls his eyes as he tells his wife he is glad to do a chore has conveyed a double message. The message that always prevails is the one conveyed by our body language.

No man is angry that feels not himself hurt.

FRANCIS BACON

How you relate nonverbally to your marriage partner is a crucial part of healthy communication. Experts estimate that about 90% of a communication is not what is said but how it is said. The *how* of communication is the nonverbal part. The box on page 95 summarizes nonverbals that are important in marital communication.

Working at having a marriage with healthy nonverbals requires developing positive day-to-day physical connection and weeding out problematic nonverbals. Nonverbals tend to be automatic; that is, we cannot easily change them just by thinking about them, unless we are professional con artists or poker players! The best way to have loving and connected nonverbals is to cultivate a daily sense of connection (see practice #2, *Make connection the norm*) so that the helpful nonverbals flow naturally from the essence of the relationship.

Calmly tell your partner one nonverbal behavior that he or she does that can be difficult for you. It might be using a certain tone, rolling the eyes, giving a particular facial expression. Give each other permission to gently point out those nonverbals when they occur, so that each of you can gradually replace them with more honoring nonverbals.

NONVERBAL COMMUNICATION

VOICE TONE: Perhaps the most important nonverbal, voice tone determines the ultimate meaning of what you say. Avoid tones that convey sarcasm, contempt, disinterest, or boredom. Maintain a tone of genuine concern and willingness to understand and work through problems.

VOLUME: The louder you speak, the less you will be heard ("You're talking so loud I can't hear what you're saying!").

EYE CONTACT: Looking someone in the eye usually communicates attention, listening, and caring. Absence of eye contact communicates distance, disengagement, or lack of concern with what the other is saying. This can, however, vary by culture.

GESTURES: Keep hand and body movements calm. Avoid pointing or using your hands in a dramatic or agitated way.

BODY POSTURE: Turning your body toward your partner rather than away creates a more honoring interaction. Making sure both of you are at the same level (both seated or both standing) prevents a sense of one person towering over the other.

FACIAL EXPRESSIONS: Be aware of how you can communicate with slight movements of facial muscles or eyes (for example, rolling eyes upward or puffing cheeks out in exasperation). Strive to keep facial expressions calm and accepting.

DISTANCE: When discussing a problem with empathic listening, sit close together in a way that helps you remember that you are intimate life partners. This makes blowing up in anger much less likely. It's easier for most people to yell at a person from a distance than up close. Sit close enough to be in one another's personal space. You're married—it's OK!

TOUCH: Some physical, affectionate contact while talking is important to maintain a sense of honoring and to soothe one another so that elevated heart rate and muscle tension don't begin to derail the discussion.

Step 6: Solve Solvable Problems

I remember receiving a call from my sister who was excited that a friend had found a way, in less than five minutes, to adjust the neck of her guitar so that it played like a dream. She had put the guitar in a closet for twenty years because it had always been so difficult to play. Hearing about that made me wonder how many things we allow to not work in our lives simply because we don't take the time to correct them. This is true of many of the issues that cause tension between spouses. Some couples fight for years over things that could be solved in a relatively short period with creative attempts at problem-solving.

John Gottman coined the term "solve solvable problems." This is his way of recognizing that not all problems in marriage are solvable (see discussion of recurring conflicts on pages 98-101). To address any of the solvable problems in your marriage, it is helpful to have a reliable model of problem-solving. Counselors often teach a model similar to the one below:

1. Define the problem (be specific and clear).
2. Brainstorm ideas for solutions. Write every idea down—no idea is discarded at this stage.
3. Eliminate the least useful ideas, narrow the list down.
4. Choose one solution and implement it.
5. Meet later to re-evaluate the solution. Repeat steps 1-5 if necessary.

It may seem like a bit much to go through these steps for each problem you encounter in your marriage. The model is not overly demanding, however, if it is built into your regular marital visioning meetings. Having a time to review tensions and brainstorm about how to live together more peacefully is an important part of continuing to refine your marital vision.

Often small problems are like the tips of icebergs. Working to solve them frequently leads to more involved discussions about another problem. Working on the problem of one or both

What we hope to do with ease, we must first learn to do with diligence.

Samuel Johnson

marriage partners being physically out of shape, for instance, can lead to discussions about the busyness of life, a commitment to eat more nutritious food, and even the desire to be more attractive to one another. Problems are often interconnected: Trying to solve one can raise others. If a couple is actively working on engaging conflict with honoring, however, there is no reason to fear getting caught in a web of interconnected problems.

> Make a list together of all the day-to-day work that is required in your household. Include everything you can think of. Separately rate from 1 to 10 how positively each of you feels about how those tasks are being completed. Talk about the items that receive lower ratings or items you rated very differently. Brainstorm new ways to approach these tasks, and then write down a new solution to try. Be sure to talk in one of your regular marital visioning meetings about how the solution is working or not working. If necessary, pick another solution and test it out. Don't expect a perfect fix right away.

STEP 7: ENJOY FEELING CONNECTED AGAIN

This is the easiest step. It is getting back to the norm of connection in your relationship. By taking time to work through the conflict, you minimize time lost to coldness, distance, or bickering. Tomorrow is another day, and it may bring you another conflict, but you have done the work today of making sure that conflict or distance is not the norm in your marriage. Step 7 isn't always about returning to your normal level of closeness. Sometimes by working through a conflict—particularly by really using the full power of empathic listening—you may understand each other more deeply and be closer than you were before the conflict.

As soon as you are aware of having given in to anger . . . repair your mistake immediately with an act of kindness to the person you have hurt.

FRANCIS DE SALES

OTHER HELPFUL PERSPECTIVES ON *BRING HONORING TO CONFLICT*

Two additional concepts beyond the seven-step model will help you bring honoring to conflict in your marriage. These have to do with how to handle conflicts that come up repeatedly in your marriage and how to get behind a conflict to the deeper discussion that needs to occur.

BRING HONORING TO RECURRENT CONFLICTS

Imagine two farmers, one who has worked the land for decades, and another, a city slicker who has just moved out to the country to enjoy the farming life. During the second spring after moving to the farm, the city slicker surveys his fields. *I just plowed these fields last spring—why must I do it again this spring?* he protests to himself. The other farmer surveys the land he has plowed repeatedly for forty years and silently gives thanks for the opportunity to continually work the land in harmony with the seasons.

Many married people act like the city slicker farmer when it comes to working the hardest and most persistent issues in their marriages. "We talked about that a month ago—why would you bring it up again?" is the type of question asked by one who believes that the fields of marital conflict should be plowed but once. In reality, every marriage has recurrent conflicts, which require us to continually engage difficult material in an honoring manner. John Gottman calls these "perpetual issues" because he believes they are never really solved. I prefer the term "recurrent"

True listening, total concentration on the other, is always a manifestation of love. An essential part of true listening is the discipline of bracketing, the temporary giving up or setting aside of one's prejudices, frames of reference, and desires so as to experience as far as possible the speaker's world from the inside, stepping inside his or her shoes.

M. SCOTT PECK

because sometimes couples can move beyond these conflicts, though usually after years of working on them.

Most married couples to whom I've presented the idea of recurrent conflicts express relief at the knowledge that every couple has long-term tensions. Most of us communicate so little about our experience of marriage with other couples that it's easy to think we're the only ones who have to keep dealing with some of the same problems over and over again.

I agree with Gottman that the goal with recurrent conflicts is not so much to solve them once and for all but to create an honoring way of engaging them each time it is necessary. Some couples may over time and almost without noticing it, live their way to where an issue that caused problems for long periods of their marriage is no longer a problem. This scenario is much more likely if honoring attempts are made to engage the issue when it comes up. If a couple allows recurrent conflicts to create repeated bad scenes or avoids any discussion of them at all, such conflicts can have a corrosive effect on the relationship.

If you are engaged to be married, you may have some difficulty determining what your recurrent conflicts are or will be in the future. If you have been married for some time, you probably have a good idea of what they are.

On the next page is a list to help you pinpoint the recurrent conflicts (perpetual issues) in your marriage If you found yourself nodding knowlingly to one or more of these, you know what recurrent conflicts are. I've never known a married couple that wasn't intimately familiar with several recurrent conflicts.

Creating an honoring interaction with recurrent conflicts means 1) accepting that you have them and 2) being committed to giving the energy it takes to engage them with honoring whenever they come up. Honoring means a willingness to hear your partner's feelings about the issue. It also means using empathic listening to make progress on dealing as effectively as possible with these tensions whenever they arise.

Let your conflict be a source of revelation . . . Disagreement is natural, conflict is part of human life. But your relationship is not a war. You do not have to win. What you have to do is learn about your beloved and about yourself. This is the primary purpose of conflict.

WILLIAM MARTIN

Most quarrels amplify a misunderstanding.

ANDRE GIDE

Gottman's Perpetual Issues List

1. *Differences in neatness and organization.* One person is neat and organized and the other is sloppy and disorganized.
2. *Differences in emotionality.* One person is very emotionally expressive and the other is not so expressive. One person also values exploring emotions more than the other.
3. *Differences in wanting time together versus time apart and alone.* One person wants more time alone than the other, who wants more time together. These reflect basic differences in wanting autonomy versus independence.
4. *Differences in optimal sexual frequency.* One person wants more sex than the other.
5. *Differences in preferred lovemaking style.* There are differences in what the two people want from lovemaking. For example, one sees intimacy as a precondition to making love, while the other sees lovemaking as a path to intimacy.
6. *Differences in approaching finances.* One person is much more financially conservative and a worrier, while the other wants to spend a lot more than the other and has a philosophy more of living in the moment.
7. *Differences with respect to kin.* One person wants more independence from kin, and the other wants more closeness.
8. *Differences in how to resolve conflict.* One person likes to openly discuss conflicts while the other would prefer to avoid them more.
9. *Differences in how to approach household chores.* For example, one person wants equal division of labor, while the other does not.
10. *Differences in how to raise and discipline children.* One person is more involved with the children than the other.
11. *Differences in how to raise and discipline children.* One person is stricter with the children than the other.
12. *Differences in how to raise and discipline children.* One person wants more gentleness and understanding used with the children than the other.
13. *Differences in punctuality.* One person is habitually late, and to the other it is important to be on time.
14. *Differences in preferred activity level.* One person prefers active physical recreation, while the other is more passive and sedentary.
15. *Differences in being people-oriented.* One person is more extraverted and gregarious than the other.
16. *Differences in preferred influence.* One person prefers to be more dominant in decision-making than the other.
17. *Differences in ambition and the importance of work.* One person is far more ambitious and oriented to work than the other.
18. *Differences with respect to religion.* One person values a religious orientation more than the other.
19. *Differences with respect to drugs and alcohol.* One person is far more tolerant of drug and alcohol use than the other.
20. *Differences in independence.* One person feels a greater need to be independent or connected than the other.
21. *Differences in excitement.* One person feels a greater need to have life be exciting or adventurous than the other.
22. *Differences in preferred lifestyle.* Partners have major differences in the way they choose to live life on an everyday basis.
23. *Differences in values.* Partners have major differences in what they value in life.
24. *Others.* You supply them here:

Reprinted by permission from John Gottman's *The Marriage Clinic*, pages 219-220.

> ⚷ Review the list of recurrent conflicts on page 100. As you do, note those that are relevant to your relationship. Compare the ones you each noted and discuss whether you feel you generally maintain an honoring interaction when these issues arise. Promise each other to do your best to use empathic listening when recurrent conflicts come up.

LOOK FOR THE DREAM BEHIND THE CONFLICT

After nearly twenty years studying and practicing psychology, I thought I'd heard every angle on how to deal with conflict. John Gottman, however, came up with a new and brilliant concept: Looking for the dream behind the conflict.

When you and your spouse dig in and hold your ground in a small squabble or full-scale marital battle, each of you is defending more than just pride or the need to be right. Usually, the positions we find worth fighting over represent ideals or dreams about which we care deeply. The problem is that the dream is so well hidden behind the conflict that our partners (and sometimes even we ourselves) cannot see it.

Suppose you are arguing about the fact that one of you prefers to go to bed early and the other is a night owl. On the surface it may appear to be simply an issue about when to retire for the evening. However, each person in such a conflict is likely to have a dream below the surface of the issue. The one who prefers to go to bed early may have the "dream" of being a well-rested person able to function at his or her best, having gotten adequate sleep. The one who argues for the right to stay up late may be addressing the "dream" or need for quiet time and personal space. A spouse who advocates that both partners should go to bed at the same time is likely speaking about a "dream" related to the need for togetherness, affection, or sexual intimacy.

Anger blows out the lamp of the mind. In the examination of a great and important question, everyone should be serene, slow-pulsed, and calm.

INGERSOLL

Half the misery in the world comes of want of courage to speak and to hear the truth plainly, and in a spirit of love.

HARRIET BEECHER STOWE

Practicing looking for the dream behind the conflict will allow you to defuse minor conflicts and make larger, recurrent ones much more workable. This practice, which requires empathic listening, allows conflict to become a gateway to greater intimacy rather than a force that gradually erodes the foundation of your love. As Gottman says, it allows you to have the deeper discussion you need to have instead of the unproductive, conflicted discussion you were having.

> ⚷ Ask your partner the following question when a conflict has come between you: "What is the dream behind the conflict for you?" This shifts the interaction from a problem focus (which is characterized by both partners defending their positions) to an understanding focus (each attempting to see what dreams are behind the conflict for the other).

To Have and to Laugh

Mr. Black Widow Gives Empathic Listening a Try

Mr. Black Widow: So, darling, let me try a reflection here to see if I'm hearing you clearly. You're saying that the next time we finish mating, you're going to kill me, lay your eggs in me, and let my carcass serve as food for our off-spring. Am I hearing you accurately?

Mrs. Black Widow: Yes, you've got it. I feel so good about you listening so empathically to my deepest feelings that I'm really in the mood for mating. What about you, darling?

For two people in a marriage to live together day after day is unquestionably the one miracle the Vatican has overlooked.

BILL COSBY

Never go to bed mad. Stay up and fight.

PHYLLIS DILLER

This makes me so sore it gets my dandruff up.

SAMUEL GOLDWYN

Key Summary Points
BRING HONORING TO CONFLICT

- Realize that conflict is a part of every marriage. How you deal with conflict will determine whether it is a path to growth and intimacy or a continual tearing at the fabric of your relationship.

- Learn the seven-step model of conflict resolution. This includes using time-outs to stop destructive interactions; reconnecting after conflict with a hug; sharing mutual, no-fault apologies; reviewing the conflict using empathic listening; and attempting to solve whatever caused the conflict.

- When using empathic listening, stay in your speaker or listener role until the speaker says, "I feel heard."

- Use "I language" when taking the speaker role in empathic listening. Avoid "you language."

- As the listener, use reflective statements to make sure you're really hearing what your partner said. Do not disagree or tell your partner he or she is wrong. Take special care to reflect the feelings your partner is expressing and to invite him or her to tell you more.

- Develop an awareness of the power of body language (nonverbals) and strive to relate to your partner nonverbally in a way that communicates honoring.

- Don't expect to solve recurrent conflicts with one or a few attempts at empathic listening. Strive for an honoring way of discussing them with one another each time they come up.

- Try to look for the dream behind the conflict. Simply ask your partner, "What is the dream behind this conflict for you?" and listen empathically.

DISCUSSION QUESTIONS

1. Review the three styles of dealing with conflict on p. 80. John Gottman says, in *The Marriage Clinic,* that two volatile persons or two avoiding persons are capable of having a stable marriage. Do you think this means that such couples should simply maintain their current approach to conflict, or is it better to learn to move toward the middle (validating)?

2. Most people want to resolve a conflict before they return to an affectionate way of relating. Do you think the idea of offering a hug, apologizing, and touching in an honoring way before you review a conflict is workable? Or do you think it's not possible to touch in an honoring way until the conflict has completely passed?

3. The idea of recurrent conflicts (pages 98-101) is a relief to most married couples. It amounts to saying that all married couples have some irreconcilable differences, and that's OK. Is accepting that some issues cannot be fixed in the short run a depressing idea to you? What does "bring honoring to recurrent conflicts" mean to you?

4. Is the idea of looking for the dream behind a conflict new to you? Can you see yourself trying that approach? What would be the main barriers to switching from an unproductive fight to a discussion about the dream each of you is defending in the conflict?

This diamond is located at the bottom of the cover image because acceptance, the core of Give up the search for the perfect lover, *is the basis upon which a great marriage rests. The couple dances around a vessel that, though cracked (imperfect), still releases the zig-zag waves of loving energy that flow from this diamond upward through* Create a shared vision *to* Walk the sacred path *(see the cover or page 14).*

GIVE UP THE SEARCH FOR THE PERFECT LOVER

SUMMARY OF THIS PRACTICE

The experience of falling in love is often based on the illusion that one has found his or her perfect match. This desire for perfect or infinite love is really a longing for God, the Infinite One. By expecting our spouses to be the One who completes us, we do harm to our marriages. A Namaste marriage is based on the realization that every human being is finite—and that marriage must be rooted in a deep acceptance of your own and your partner's strengths and limitations. Paradoxically, genuine acceptance frees your partner to become his or her best self. If you try to change your partner, you will provoke resistance to change. If you accept your partner as is, you will create a relationship in which true growth is possible.

SPIRITUAL FOCUS FOR THIS PRACTICE

Only in God will my soul be at rest.

Psalm 62: 1

*I*f you're engaged, you may still be under the illusion that you have found your perfect match. If you are married, you know you haven't. We live in a culture that glorifies the process of falling in love but gives us little clear appreciation of the actual experience of living out a lifetime commitment of love in marriage.

Listen to love songs on the radio. So many of them include the idea of "you complete me" or a similar romantic notion. This persistent model of "true love" is a myth. God is the only one who can complete any of us, and your partner is not God, though he or she is made in God's image and can shine with Divine energy. Marriage becomes extraordinary when we move beyond the ill-founded hope for perfect love into a commitment to making our real, human marriage the best that it can be.

Give up the search for the perfect lover—which is all about accepting and affirming your partner "as is"—is placed in the bottom diamond on the cover image because acceptance is the soil in which a great marriage grows. We are called back to acceptance and affirmation over and over in marriage. We learn as we gather wisdom that personal and marital growth can only occur if grounded in acceptance.

The myth of perfect love is destructive because it creates a passive orientation to marriage. Instead of realizing that a good marriage is created out of the daily loving behaviors of the couple, we expect it to unfold beautifully of its own perfectly programmed accord. When things begin to go sour, most couples don't know what to do. Plan A was to have a perfect marriage, and there's no plan B. So the marriage just drifts along; the man and woman get busy with careers or raising a family or both—all the while hoping that everything will eventually fall into place, without any clear blueprint for how that might happen. In time, many couples just let go of the dream of perfect love and replace it with an uneasy existence in a relationship that seems to have settled for the lowest common denominator.

The idea of "soul mates" is common today. A soul mate is presumably a partner who fits your soul, your whole person, like

Until I am essentially united with God, I can never have full rest or real happiness.

JULIAN OF NORWICH

Even a great marriage leaves some part of each partner unsatisfied . . . In a good marriage the partners accept that they can't have everything, that some wishes will always remain unmet.

JUDITH WALLERSTEIN
AND SANDRA BLAKESLEE

a glove. I believe the concept of soul mates is misleading and that "soul companions" is a preferable term. A soul companion is a person with whom you choose to journey through life, a partner who accepts and affirms you and may challenge you to grow personally and spiritually, though not always in the ways you'd prefer. "Soul companion" leaves room for the sometimes-challenging practice of acceptance, whereas "soul mate" seems to imply that acceptance should never be difficult because the fit is perfect.

My parents had one of the best marriages I've ever seen. For forty-eight years they were faithful to one another, raised eight children, went to church and prayed together, and embarked on wonderful adventures. Yet their relationship had its recurring tensions, its times of crisis, its seasons of loneliness. They bumped into the need for the spiritual practice of acceptance on almost a daily basis.

Both the joys and the challenges of marriage are part of the whole that make up this sacred way of living. Wanting only the easy or fun part of the experience is neither a realistic hope nor a path to personal or spiritual growth. One of the most challenging parts is accepting another person who is and always will be fundamentally different from you. The late Urban Steinmetz, in *Strangers, Lovers, Friends* went so far as to say that one's spouse is always part stranger, a person one never totally understands or figures out. A prevailing attitude of acceptance goes a long way toward helping spouses deal with tensions that result not necessarily from specific conflicts but just from the fact that they are different, unique individuals.

Give up the search for the perfect lover, then, implies allowing your marriage to be human, to have both pure joy and pesky problems, good times and bad, closeness and tensions that need ongoing healing. We need a model of marriage that not only makes it OK to be human, but recognizes that fidelity to dealing with the challenge of acceptance in married life is a major part of what can make a marriage extraordinary. This is a spiritual practice because it entails the ongoing effort to give unconditional love.

But what is the basic truth of all marriages? All of us marry strangers; no matter how long we search for a compatible mate . . .

URBAN STEINMETZ

I am not at all the person you and I took me for.

JANE WELSH CARLYLE

Too many married people expect their partner to give that which only God can give, namely an eternal ecstasy.

FULTON J. SHEEN

I honor you.

I honor you,
my soul.

I honor you,
my soul
companion, as you are.

I honor you,
my soul
companion, as you are
Divinity in disguise.

Many couples still promise on their wedding days "to honor and love." It seems, though, that love gets all the press, and the concept of honoring is largely ignored. Give up the search for the perfect lover is an ongoing spiritual practice in marriage that 1) draws us back to the power of honoring our human lovers with acceptance and affirmation and 2) reminds us that the only Perfect Lover is God.

PRACTICING
GIVE UP THE SEARCH FOR THE PERFECT LOVER IN YOUR MARRIAGE

Note: This chapter encourages a basic attitude of acceptance and affirmation of your marriage partner, despite differences that cause tension. Clearly, however, there are behaviors or situations (such as alcoholism, drug abuse, lying, or violence) of a more serious nature that should not be affirmed, accepted, or tolerated. See Appendix B (page 208) for a discussion of serious toxic behaviors in marriage that should be eliminated, not accepted.

KNOW YOUR TEMPLATE FOR THE PERFECT LOVER

While the ultimate prototype for the perfect lover that we carry in our minds is God, in actuality our expectations for a marriage partner are formed by our experience of human love long before we meet our spouse. If you had a good relationship with a parent, you are likely to want a future spouse to be like that parent. If you had a difficult relationship with a parent, you are likely to want your spouse not to be like that parent. Your mother and father usually have the strongest shaping influence on what you look for or hope to avoid in a partner. However, other people, such as stepparents, siblings, ex-spouses, former girl- or boyfriends, or important teachers also can affect your template of the perfect lifetime partner.

An internalized template of desired attributes or traits sounds like it would be helpful, and to some degree it can shape your choice of a good marriage partner. The problem occurs when we expect another person to fit the template perfectly (which never happens). When you begin wondering why your partner doesn't

. . . love is never simple, . . . it brings with it struggles of the past and hopes for the future . . . it is loaded with material that may be remotely—if at all— connected to the person who is the apparent object of love.

THOMAS MOORE

When you love someone all your saved up wishes start coming out.

ELIZABETH BOWEN

set the table the way it should be set (that is, the way your mother or father set it), you know that the template is working overtime stirring up trouble in your marriage.

How can we be sure that no one in this life will match the perfect template in our minds? A bit of math might help. Suppose you have six traits you're looking for in a spouse, and each person in the population has a 10% chance of having each trait. How many people will match all six traits? The answer is: one in a million. In reality, most people have a much longer list of desired traits (where does "Always throws socks in the hamper" go on the list?). If the list is only ten traits long, the chances are one in ten billion that anyone on the planet will match all ten. That, of course, is more people than are alive. If the list is only eleven traits long, then the odds are one in one hundred billion, which is more people than have ever walked the face of the earth throughout all history! My personal list of desired traits runs at least fifty items long, which means there might be an alien in a faraway galaxy that would suit me just fine.

Giving up the search for the perfect lover involves being aware that you may carry certain expectations from past relationships that can make it difficult to accept your partner "as is." These expectations are far more powerful when we are not conscious of them. For instance, you may be upset at your spouse without realizing that you are making yourself upset by holding on to a rigid template or image of who your spouse should be. When we can say to ourselves, "OK—that's an expectation from the past; let go and accept what is true in this relationship," we have a better chance of nurturing our marriage with acceptance and affirmation.

Another reality of the template for the perfect lover is that it is shaped at an unconscious level by some of the hurtful experiences of our early lives. We seek not only a person with the *positive* qualities we desire, but one with the *negative* attributes that will give us the opportunity to re-experience and heal some of the core wounds of early life. For more on this important idea, read Harville Hendrix's book *Getting the Love You Want*.

The idea is not the reality, the idea "wine" is not wine, the idea "woman" is not this woman.

ANTHONY DE MELLO

&—➤ Take a few minutes for each of you to make a list of the people (mom, dad, stepparents) who shaped your ideas about men/women, husbands/wives, and marriage. For each person, list any positive traits that you hoped a marriage partner would have and any negative traits that you hoped a marriage partner would not have. Discuss your lists with one another and how your "template" (the image you carry inside of the partner you think you want or need) affects your ability to accept your partner "as is."

ACCEPT YOUR PARTNER'S PREFERENCE FOR INTROVERSION OR EXTROVERSION (I OR E)

There are many ways we could look at common differences in married partners for the sake of illustrating the importance of acceptance. I have chosen to focus on the four dimensions of the Myers-Briggs Type Indicator (MBTI) because it is one of the most useful personality inventories for understanding some of the difficulties that married couples encounter.

The Myers-Briggs goes back several decades. It was originally based on Jungian ideas of personality structure, but today it is interpreted as a way to understand an individual's distinct way of being in the world. When a person takes the MBTI, he or she receives a four-letter code that indicates a personality type. Each of the four letters represents the person's preference for one end of a continuum. The four dimensions are:

Everything in life that we really accept undergoes a change.

KATHERINE MANSFIELD

Extroversion	(E)	vs.	Introversion	(I)
Sensible Realism	(S)	vs.	INtuitive Idealism	(N)
Thinking	(T)	vs.	Feeling	(F)
Judicious Organization	(J)	vs.	Predictable Spontaneity	(P)

Eliminate the pressure to change and you will both find true joy.

WILLIAM MARTIN

A person can score anywhere from one extreme to the other on each of these four dimensions. (Each dimension will be explained in its own section below.) There are sixteen possible four-letter combinations that make up distinct ways of experiencing the world and living one's life. Note that instead of using "sensing" and "intuiting" as the actual MBTI does for the second dimension, I have coined the terms "sensible realist" and "intuitive idealist." Likewise, the labels I have chosen for the fourth dimension are my own because the terms on the actual Myers-Briggs confuse many people. More organized people in Myers-Briggs terminology are said to be "judging" (J) and more spontaneous people are called "perceiving" (P). I've preserved the letter designations from the original inventory but have tried to use labels that make more sense for our purposes.

Let's consider the first dimension: Extroverted (E) versus Introverted (I). Put simply, people differ on how much they like to be around other people. Strong extroverts glory in being around people; they become energized by being in groups or gatherings. The extroverts on the planet are the ones who throw most of the parties and organize most of the social events. Introverts, on the other hand, can handle group interaction but prefer to do so for a limited time. They are energized most by space and quiet. They are the ones who love reading, the ones most likely to write the books, the poetry, to be on friendly terms with silence.

A marriage may have two introverts, two extroverts, or one of each. Two introverts may find themselves feeling isolated at times, not developing an active social life. Two extroverts may be good at keeping busy with others but not as good at finding quiet, peaceful times together.

This dimension of the MBTI can shed light on certain conflicts in marriage, particularly around a couple's social life or the amount of time each person wants to spend with his or her own friends (in person or on the telephone). Some couples may struggle to determine how much time they should spend with each other—extroverts wanting more together time, introverts wanting more space.

The key insight here is that neither introversion nor extroversion is the right way to be. Both are legitimate personality preferences that tend to be stable. Trying to forcibly change this aspect of your partner will provoke resentment. Over time, however, strong introverts can learn the importance of regular social interaction, and strong extroverts can learn to value silence and reflection.

Here's a telling and rather humorous story from our marriage about the I-E dimension and acceptance. On the morning of the first day of the current millennium, Claudia and I got up early to see the sunrise. We stood there on our deck with our steaming cups of coffee in total silence for fifteen minutes as that great fireball slowly appeared behind a screen of silhouetted trees on the horizon. Then I turned to her and said, "Wow, you're really a quiet person, aren't you?" I knew that I enjoyed quiet, but my mother had always been a very social, extroverted woman, and I had spent our whole marriage believing deep down that my wife's natural preference for quiet was a stage that she would outgrow. On that first day of the millennium, fifteen years into our marriage, I began to accept the introverted part of my wife "as is."

I love criticism just so long as it's unqualified praise.

NOEL COWARD

⚷ Determine whether each of you is more introverted or extroverted. Place your own and your partner's initials on the continuum below to indicate the strength of your introversion or extroversion:

|—————————————————|—————————————————|

Introverted   Extroverted

Try saying this to each other: "I affirm you as an introverted (or extroverted) person. I accept you as you are." This may sound silly or canned, but for some couples such a statement can be an important step toward acceptance that can considerably ease longstanding tension.

ACCEPT YOUR PARTNER'S PREFERENCE FOR SENSIBLE REALISM OR iNTUITIVE IDEALISM (S OR N)

Did you ever know someone who could tell you the color and pattern of the wallpaper in a mere acquaintance's house, based on one visit ten years ago? On the other hand, did you ever know someone who couldn't tell you the color of the wallpaper in his or her own kitchen? The first person is a strong "sensible realist" (S). These people are tuned in to the world around them. They observe and take in the world constantly. The content of their thoughts at any time is most likely to be determined by what they are observing or what is happening around them. The second kind of person is a strong "iNtuitive idealist" (N, to distinguish it from the "I" used for introverted). He or she pays relatively little attention to the observable world, preferring instead to focus on the ideas constantly generated by and circulating in his or her own mind.

My father was an intuitive idealist. When he was deep in thought, you could practically shout in his ear, and it would be thirty seconds before the message interrupted the flow of his thoughts. My mother tends toward sensible realism. One of the minor recurrent tensions of their marriage was Mom telling Dad that he could not go out in public the way he was dressed. Sensible realists are tuned into clothing far more than intuitive idealists, who may see clothing mainly as something to cover nakedness and keep warm.

This S—N dimension may be a bit difficult for some readers to understand at first. For others, it can illuminate a formidable challenge that has caused long-term marital conflict. I have seen couples consider divorce primarily because of their difficulty accepting their differences on this S—N dimension. This is because intuitive idealists may define intimacy as talking about the creative wanderings of their minds, the endless possibilities they see for the things in which they are most interested. Sensible realists, on the other hand, prefer to talk about day-to-day or concrete things because their minds are good at observing each moment as it unfolds.

We start from what is, not from what should be.

ROSAMUND ZANDER

Imagine the conversation. She, the intuitive idealists, says: "I've been pondering this amazing new way to solve the problem of global warming." He, the sensible realist, responds with, "That's great. By the way, did you remember to gas up the car? It was on empty this morning." After years of such misconnections—she thinking her husband doesn't really care about her excitements, he thinking his wife doesn't care enough about his day-to-day concerns—a couple can begin to grow distant. Some people begin to look for another person who can talk about the kinds of things they most want to discuss.

Give up the search for the perfect lover means accepting your partner's sensible realist or intuitive idealist preference just as it is. It also means trying to understand your partner's preference so that you can do a better job of engaging her or him in conversation.

If you insist on happiness you create misery . . . If you insist on certain behavior you insure its opposite.

WILLIAM MARTIN

☞ Place your initials on the line below to indicate where you think each of you falls on the S—N dimension:

|—————————————————|—————————————————|

Sensible   Intuitive
Realist   Idealist

Discuss whether your parents were primarily sensate (focused on the external, observable world) or intuitive (focused on the inner world). Did any difference on that dimension cause them tension? What about your relationship? Are you two sensible realists, two intuitive idealists, or one of each? Do you ever find conversation difficult because of the different ways your minds operate? How can you do a better job of accepting any difference on this dimension and learning to engage your partner more effectively in conversation she or he enjoys?

ACCEPT YOUR PARTNER'S PREFERENCE FOR THINKING OR FEELING (T OR F)

This is a big one for many couples! Whereas the dimension of Sensible realism versus iNtuitive idealism concerns where we get the thoughts that preoccupy us on a daily basis (from our environment or our own minds), the Thinking-Feeling dimension is about how we process the content of our minds and our lives. Thinkers prefer logic and problem-solving; feelers prefer to go with their gut.

Does the following situation sound familiar to you? One partner is upset, wants to just vent some emotions, have his or her spouse listen without solving anything. The other partner reacts with an effort to find a solution to make the feelings go away as soon as possible. Such is the dance that feelers and thinkers often do with each other.

This dimension of personality also shows up in how people make decisions that affect their lives. Thinkers are likely to make lists of pros and cons and try to determine the most logical plan of action. Feelers make decisions based on what feels right, not on logic. The tension between these two approaches can arise in any marriage when big decisions need to be made.

However, the day-to-day difficulty in this area is usually the difference in the amount of time thinkers and feelers want to spend talking about feelings or ideas. Feeling types define intimacy as the ability to share and talk about deep *feelings*. Thinkers are more likely to define intimacy as sharing excitement about *ideas*.

Again, we must start with acceptance—an acknowledgement that our partner is different, not wrong or defective—if he or she does not match our preferred position on the Thinking-Feeling continuum. An intentional (on purpose) approach to honoring a partner's preferred style would be to make both thinking and feeling part of the couple's way of connecting. For the feeler, this might mean allowing the thinker to be a mentor in using rational, logical thinking to deal with emotional situations. For the thinker, honoring might mean learning to become aware of and share one's own feelings and listen genuinely to a partner's feelings.

Listening is a form of accepting.

STELLA TERRILL MANN

> ⚿ Each of you put your own and your partner's initials on the continuum below to indicate where you think (or feel!) each of you falls.
>
> |————————————|————————————|
>
> Thinking   Feeling
>
> Now discuss how you can be more intentional about honoring any differences between you on this dimension.

ACCEPT YOUR PARTNER'S PREFERENCE FOR JUDICIOUS ORGANIZATION OR PREDICTABLE SPONTANEITY (J OR P)

I remember my mother trying to change me from a "predictably spontaneous" person (P) into a "judiciously organized" person (J). Sometimes she had me make my bed repeatedly on the same day to learn that making one's bed is important. After years of that J training, I moved into my own apartment at age twenty-one and gloried in *not* making my bed. Her prolonged and well-intended effort to change me had failed!

When I took the Myers-Briggs Type Indicator the first time, I learned that I was about as P as a P could be. It wasn't until I was trying to run a mental health center that the real world gave me the motivation I needed to develop better organizational skills.

When Claudia and I were first married, my idea of doing the dishes was to leave them stacked in the sink until late at night. This really bugged her, and I eventually learned to do them immediately after the meal. Buying a little television set so that I could watch the news while I did dishes helped a lot. If technology can help a marriage, why not?

Judiciously organized (J) types tend to be neat, timely, reliable and planful. They have a high need for "closure," which means that when they begin something, they usually finish it before starting something else. They like to make lists and check things

If you can learn to take delight in what seems flawed and wrong in each other, you create the atmosphere that enables growth and change.

WILLIAM MARTIN

119

Why does a woman work ten years to change a man's habits and then complain that he's not the man she married?

BARBARA STREISAND

off. They have a strong preference for cleanliness and order. Predictably spontaneous (P) types, on the other hand, prefer to do what their energy indicates at the moment, not what a schedule or list tells them they should be doing. They do not share the J type's need for closure. They are comfortable doing many things at once and leaving them in an unfinished state. They can tolerate disorderliness, lateness, and some degree of messiness. It's just not a high priority for them to keep things spic and span.

These types often marry each other and spend years fighting about this J-P dimension. In Myers-Briggs circles, the most frequently-heard pun is, "If you'll respect my J-ness, I'll respect your P-ness." As silly as that sounds, working with differences on this dimension really does begin with respect and acceptance of the other person just the way he or she is.

This is an area in which tensions can be minimized if both people learn to move to the middle. J people in particular—who often see cleanliness as next to godliness and therefore have great difficulty accepting a partner who is not neat and orderly—need to learn to accept a different style. In return, a P who is married to a J will greatly help the marriage by learning to develop a neater and more organized approach that closes the distance a bit between the spouses on this dimension.

Each of you place your own and your partner's initials on the line below to indicate where you think each of you falls on the J-P continuum:

|⊢——————————————————|——————————————————⊣|

Judiciously   Predictably
Organized   Spontaneous

Now discuss the ways in which you see any differences causing tension between you. Talk about how each of you can work on accepting the other person's J or P style—and how you can learn to honor your partner's preference by moving somewhat in her or his direction on the continuum.

DON'T JUST HABITUATE—CELEBRATE!

One of the realities of the human brain that works against a consistent acceptance and honoring of our marriage partners is called habituation. This simply means that we get used to things. Aspects of life that used to bring us joy and delight can become familiar or even boring. Old fashions are replaced by new ones; new movies are more intriguing than ones we've already seen; and yes, a spouse's traits that used to attract us can lose their luster or even begin to turn us off.

Habituation is a gradual process that can erode the sense of specialness about one's partner or marriage. The woman who was attracted to her handsome, spontaneous, carefree fiance may now find her husband's lack of organization irksome. A man who initially found his wife's high degree of intelligence attractive may now feel distant from or threatened by her because she's "too intellectual."

How can we learn to celebrate instead of habituate? How can we continue to appreciate rather than take for granted the traits that first drew us together? A commitment to regularly affirming each other "as is" is key. The more we affirm our partner's basic goodness, the more we will experience such energy in return. Such affirmation is the opposite of continually criticizing a partner because he or she is different. Such basic acceptance can motivate partners to be flexible in trying to respect each other's preferences. It's easier to make a move from an extreme end of a personality continuum (such as one of the four Myers-Briggs dimensions) when we feel accepted for who we are. It's basically a "I'll work on accepting you and trying to respect your preferred style, and please do the same for me" exchange between partners.

Genius . . . means little more than the faculty of perceiving in an unhabitual way.

WILLIAM JAMES

> Each of you write down three qualities of your partner that you don't celebrate as much as you did when you first fell in love. Discuss how you can celebrate at least one of those qualities with each other sometime soon.

Love finds its soul in its feelings of incompleteness, impossibility, and imperfection.

THOMAS MOORE

The soul hardly ever realizes it, but whether he is a believer or not, his loneliness is really a homesickness for God.

HUBERT VAN ZELLER

Prayer is . . . a longing of the soul.

MOHANDAS GANDHI

ACCEPT LONGING AS A PART OF BEING HUMAN

We began this chapter on *Give up the search for the perfect lover* by acknowledging that only God is the Perfect Lover. Even Namaste marriages are full of the celebration of love and the awareness that marriage includes times of loneliness and longing.

Most of us tend to think of longing as a negative—as a bothersome awareness of a lack of something we deeply desire. If we begin to think of longing as one of the best reminders of our deeply spiritual nature, we can accept it as part of the package of being human. We are finite creatures with infinite longings. Expecting marriage to fill up our infinite longings only makes it easier for us to dishonor our sacred commitment to a life partner and think that love could be more perfect with someone else. The idea that marriage can complete us is an illusion. We learn about love by loving the human being we've committed to love and accepting the longing for perfect love as a form of connection to God, not a sign that we need a different partner.

⚷ Get in touch with your own experience of longing by writing "I long for . . ." and completing it at least three different ways. Don't complete the sentence with material things you want, such as, "I long for a new car." Try to get in touch with some of the deepest longings of your soul—longing for pure love, perfect acceptance, the childhood you didn't have, the childhood you did have, a sense of inner peace, a sense of financial security, an experience of lasting happiness. Talk about what you wrote with your partner. Discuss how to let it be OK that marriage cannot remove the experience of longing from human life. Set the norm that your marriage will be extraordinary, in part because you will be open with each other about your experience of longing, not because your marriage will remove all of your longing.

To Have and to Laugh

Should Penny and Tip Get Married?

Penny (left shoe): Oh Tip, I'm so glad I found Mr. Right, that you and I are both 10's, that we're going to tie the knot, that we are sole mates! But what are those unsightly pockmarks on your leather uppers? I just noticed them. I think you know I place a high priority on a perfect, smooth, polished complexion. And why is your tongue always hanging out when you look at me?

Tip (right shoe): First of all, I'm actually a size 10.5. Second, Penny, let's face it—you're a loafer, and I'm getting worn down just thinking about being the sole provider in this relationship. Maybe if you weren't a loafer, I wouldn't be living on a shoestring. And I can't help that I have holes in the surface of my uppers—I'm a wing tip, for crying out loud! It gets tiring being the only dress shoe in this relationship. Why do you have to be so casual all the time?

And my tongue hanging out? Well, Penny, I guess, despite all our differences, I still have eyes for you!

I hate housework! You make the beds, you do the dishes—and six months later you have to start all over again.

JOAN RIVERS

<u>Key Summary Points</u>
GIVE UP THE SEARCH FOR THE PERFECT LOVER

◆ A Namaste marriage is rooted in a fundamental acceptance and affirmation of one's partner "as is." This is a spiritual practice because it entails the ongoing effort to offer unconditional love.

◆ Some toxic behaviors should not be accepted (see Appendix B, page 208).

◆ Our expectations for our partners are affected by our relationships with parents and others during our growing up years. The list of things we look for or want to avoid in a partner form an ideal image or template that can make acceptance of our real life partner more difficult.

◆ Couples can experience tension because of their differences on the four dimensions of the Myers-Briggs Type Indicator. In each case, accepting one's partner "as is" is the starting point for reducing tension. When we give and receive acceptance, we are more likely to be willing to be flexible about personality conflicts for the good of the relationship.

◆ Habituation is the process that can turn traits that initially attracted partners into traits that drive them apart. Remember to celebrate the goodness of who your partner is instead of taking her or his gifts for granted.

◆ Accepting one's partner "as is" implies that longing is a normal part of marriage. Marriage is not capable of fulfilling all of our longings, but it can give us a soul companion on the journey to God, the Perfect Lover for whom we all long.

DISCUSSION QUESTIONS

1. Do you think it's true that many couples hope for perfect love but don't have a clear sense of how to create a loving real-life relationship with an imperfect human being on a daily basis?

2. Your whole marriage is an opportunity to learn to accept your partner as he or she is. Does this slow, life-long process of acceptance and honoring seem boring next to the concept of finding the perfect match?

3. Acceptance of your partner "as is" does not mean merely being resigned to his or her differentness. It means learning to celebrate differences, exploring your partner's preferred ways of being, and stretching yourself a bit to enter her or his world. How do you do this (or plan to do this) in your marriage?

4. Letting go of the illusion of perfect love opens us to the possibility of learning how to love another finite human being over many years. Where does the feeling of being "in love" fit in this model of marriage? Which is more attractive to you: remaining "in love" or remaining in a deeply loving relationship?

The artist has gotten playful in this depiction of Work on the "I" in marriage. He's represented the scripture passage on the next page by placing an "I"-shaped log in an eyeball. The two seed-pod-like plant shapes represent the importance of both marriage partners continuing to grow by working on their own habit energies.

WORK ON THE "I" IN MARRIAGE

SUMMARY OF THIS PRACTICE

Coaches are fond of reminding their players that there is no "I" in "team." There is, however, an "I" in marriage, right there near the center of the word. In fact, the word could be spelled "marrIIage" because there are really two "I's" in a marriage. Every married person has some habit energies (patterns of thinking, feeling, or behaving) that help the relationship grow and some that hold it back. Each of us has areas in which she or he can become a better person and marriage partner. Our marriages go much better when we keep growing as individuals. Continuing to work on yourself is where you have the most leverage for improving your marriage.

SPIRITUAL FOCUS
FOR THIS PRACTICE

Why do you notice the splinter in your brother's eye but do not notice the log in your own?

Luke 6: 41

*M*y father's last words are a treasure to all who knew him well. Just before going into a coma, he told one of his grandchildren: "You can never be other than who you are, but you can always be better than who you are now." His words express the delicate balance between accepting our essential nature "as is" and working always to become a better version of ourselves. We need the ability to hold these two seemingly opposing ideas (self-acceptance and self-improvement) in a healthy tension, realizing that both contain truths necessary to our growth as individuals and marriage partners.

Creating a Namaste marriage is not possible if you expect all the work to be done on the marriage itself. The basic building blocks of marriage are the two individuals. These separate persons do not disappear when you say "I do." No sports franchise can have a winning team without strong individual players who continue to improve their skills. Likewise, creating the best version of your relationship will require two individuals committed to working on personal growth throughout the entire marriage. Focusing on individual goals for becoming a better person is not self-centered. It is a great gift to your marriage.

The day-to-day reality of working on the "I" in marriage involves addressing patterns that were developed long before we ever met our spouses. In the years prior to marriage, every person develops what spiritual writer and monk Thich Nhat Hanh calls "habit energies"—ways of behaving, feeling, or thinking that are well-established and require considerable intentional energy to change.

When two people marry, their habit energies coincide nicely in some areas and clash in others. As we learned in the last chapter, a man who is used to keeping everything neat might marry a woman who is comfortable with disorder. Neither person is wrong for being the way she or he is, but each can contribute to a better marriage by working with her or his habit energies. Any seasoned married person knows that insisting that the other per-

The curious paradox is that when I accept myself just as I am, then I can change.

CARL ROGERS

128

son be the one who does all the growing or changing only creates more problems.

In building a Namaste marriage, we commit to allowing the marriage to be a school a love. Many of the lessons in that school have to do with healing some of the wounds or unfinished business of our early years that continue to influence our lives through our habit energies. Marriage has an uncanny way of allowing us to re-experience our early life issues. A man who felt like a disappointment to his parents as a boy might carry the fear that his wife will find him lacking and leave him for another man. A woman who did not feel recognized in her family for her intelligence might be unusually sensitive to her husband's remarks about what she says, reads, or accomplishes. A husband who was the favored child of his parents might find his wife's admiration of him insufficient. Sexual messages or experiences from early life can help create habit energies that become barriers to a truly celebratory experience of sex in marriage. Our personal history is important in marriage because it affects who we are now. The habitual patterns of behavior, thought, and emotion that determine how we relate to ourselves and our marriage partners are rooted in the rich soil of our life stories.

Habit is the easiest way to be wrong again.

LAURENCE PETER

If you would love, love and be lovable.

BENJAMIN FRANKLIN

The beauty of marriage, though, is that we also bring positive habit energies and can teach them to one another. When we were first married, for instance, Claudia taught me that it was possible to respond to tension with affection and honoring. Her gentle habit energy helped me see and work on the volatile habit energy that I had modeled after my father's response to stress. If we allow a process of mutual mentoring (see page 148) to occur, we can experience the remarkable school of love that is marriage—a school in which each spouse is a primary teacher for her or his partner.

The "default" mode for dealing with marital stress is to look for what is wrong with the other person. *Work on the "I" in marriage* reverses that approach. Your greatest leverage to create a better marriage is to work on your own habit energies.

Nested Meditation

You don't see me.

You don't see me
like I am.

You don't see me
like I am
you.

You don't see me
like I am.
You
see me like you are.

We think we perceive the world objectively, as it is, but we do not. We see the world as we are—which means we often see through non-conscious beliefs that we project onto others. Our habitual ways of behaving, thinking, and feeling can color our perception of our spouses just as if we were wearing rose- or dark-tinted glasses. If we want to be better able to see and accept our marriage partners as they are, we need to work continually on our own habit energies.

> # PRACTICING
> ## *WORK ON THE "I" IN MARRIAGE*
> # IN YOUR MARRIAGE

A CLOSER LOOK AT "HABIT ENERGIES"

A habit energy is any well-rehearsed pattern of behaving, thinking, or feeling. It is something we have done, thought, or felt enough times that it is now on "automatic pilot." Our habit energies shape our day-to-day experience of life and our relationships with ourselves and others.

How many different habit energies are there? I think their number is unlimited because any sequence of behaviors, thoughts, or feelings can become habitual, and the number of such possible sequences is endless. You may have a habit energy about how you tie your shoes, what time of day you bathe or shower, or how you prefer to do things in the kitchen. You may have habitual thoughts about men, women, work, sex, success, or any other aspect of life that help determine your experience. Your moods may, in part, be habitual energies that seem to have a life of their own.

Anytime we think the problem is "out there," that thought is the problem.
STEPHEN COVEY

The box on page 132 presents just a few of the habit energies that can have an impact on the health of a marriage. Notice that the habit energies are presented as ends of a continuum. Every habit has its opposite, which is why habit energies can create conflict in marriage. No one has the best version of every habit, and no couple has an exact alignment of habit energies.

> ⌐━━ In the box on page 132, circle the habit energies you have that you feel affect your marriage for better or worse. Discuss these with your spouse. Pick one that you would like to work on and make a commitment to a small, measurable, achievable change intended to improve your marriage.

SOME HABIT ENERGIES
THAT MAY AFFECT YOUR MARRIAGE

Behavioral habit energies:

Neatness	Messiness
Timeliness	Tardiness
Talkative	Quiet
Early riser	Late riser
Extroverted	Introverted
Risk-taking	Risk-avoiding
Regular exercise	Irregular/no exercise
Affectionate	Not affectionate
Sexual initiator	Sexually passive

Thinking habit energies:

Self-accepting	Self-critical
Accepting of others	Critical of others
Optimist	Pessimist
Possibility thinker	Reality-based thinker
Other-centered	Preoccupied with self
Prone to exaggerate	Prone to under-react
Flexible opinions	Rigid opinions

Emotional habit energies:

Often happy	Often melancholy
Calm	Anger/anxiety prone
Secure	Insecure/jealous
Not easily hurt	Easily hurt
Strong sexual desire	Weak sexual desire
Grateful	Ungrateful
Emotionally open	Emotionally private

THE FOUR HARBINGERS OF HAPPINESS

In his research, John Gottman has identified four corrosive patterns in marriage that he calls "the four horsemen of the apocalypse." If you spend a lot of time living out of these four habit energies, they will gut your marriage and leave it devoid of love. The four horsemen are: criticism, defensiveness, stonewalling (withdrawal or cold-shouldering), and contempt. When viewed as habit energies, it is immediately apparent that each of the four horsemen has an opposite. I have dubbed these opposites "the four harbingers of happiness."

Criticism is a habit energy that leads a person to constantly find fault with his or her mate. The criticizer thinks he or she is pointing out problems in a partner that are holding the relationship back, not realizing that the criticism itself is the bigger problem. The first harbinger of happiness, then, is *affirmation*. The opposite of criticism, affirmation is a regular habit of building up one's partner with genuine words and deeds that convey: "You are beautiful, you are special."

Criticism is the cancer of relationships.

WILLIAM MARTIN

Defensiveness, the second horseman of the apocalypse, is the habit of refusing to accept a partner's influence, consider his or her opinions, or respond to his or her concerns. It is founded on a habit of thinking that personal security means being right or perfect at all times and seeing others who find fault with us as enemies. The second harbinger of happiness, the opposite of defensiveness, is *openness*—the willingness to listen, to take one's partner's concerns seriously, even to allow one's partner to be a teacher in the ongoing school of married love.

Gottman's third horseman is stonewalling, or what I call withdrawal. This is the habit of responding to conflict by not responding, by pulling away and giving the cold shoulder, by treating the other person for a time as if he or she does not exist. The opposite habit, and the third harbinger of happiness, is *reconnection*. Marriage gives frequent opportunities to choose between distancing in hurt or reconnecting with compassion and forgiveness. Partners in Namaste marriages develop the latter habit.

Every time you find yourself irritated or angry with someone, the one to look at is not that person but yourself. The question to ask is not, "What's wrong with this person," but "What does this irritation tell me about myself" ... Initially look into the very real possibility that the reason why this person's ... so called defects annoy you is that you have them yourself.

ANTHONY DE MELLO

The fourth horseman of the apocalypse is contempt. Whereas every marriage has some of the first three horsemen, Gottman indicates that only very troubled marriages have contempt—a pervasive pattern of degrading one's partner through abusive language or behavior. The counterpart of this destructive habit, and the final harbinger of happiness, is *honoring*—the constant communication that one's partner is unconditionally worthy of honor and respect.

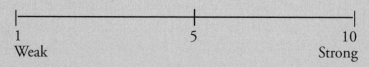 Each of you place an A for affirmation, O for openness, R for reconnection, and H for honoring on the 1-10 scale below to indicate how strong you feel each harbinger of happiness is in your marriage.

1	5	10
Weak		Strong

Talk about these ratings with one another. Be sure to use the basic skills of *Bring honoring to conflict* (good nonverbals, empathic listening—see pages 87-95). Allow your partner to give you feedback on your ratings, but remember not to be defensive!

MALE AND FEMALE ROLES HABIT ENERGIES

The roles that you witnessed between your parents (or primary caregivers) were absorbed deep into your brain and became part of the template for what you expect or hope to avoid in your own marriage. Enlightened attitudes about the equality of women and men do not go as far as we might hope to ensure that couples will not have conflict about male and female roles. In day-to-day married life, wives and husbands often act out of longstanding habit energies that determine how they feel roles in marriage should go.

A habit is essential to human living. How would we ever walk or speak or drive a car unless we relied on habit? But habits must be limited to things mechanical—not to love . . . Who wants to be loved from a habit?

ANTHONY DE MELLO

Usually both partners can work on habit energies when it comes to minimizing tension over household work. One who has a tendency to nag or be critical can work on that. Another who has the habit of not doing enough can make specific commitments to do more—and then follow through. Whoever is the neater of the two partners may need to work on a habit energy that sets overly-specific standards for how everything must be done. Those standards, applied to each household chore, are really just one person's habit of how that particular chore should be done. Openness to another's standards is important.

The issue of male and female roles in marriage goes way beyond household chores. Who works outside the home, who gets up to do nighttime feedings of infants, who plans the social calendar, who initiates sex—all of these and many more can involve our habitual ways of thinking about how women and men relate. A couple committed to creating a Namaste marriage will talk openly about all aspects of male and female roles so that both feel they are living out a shared vision of who should do what in the marriage.

Habit with him was all the test of truth; "It must be right, I've done it from my youth."

GEORGE CRABBE

Habits are first cobwebs, then cables.

SPANISH PROVERB

Have each of you rate the following areas from 1 (no shared vision) to 10 (completely shared vision) regarding how together you are on your interpretation of male and female roles:

	RATING
Doing household chores (inside)	_____
Doing household chores (outside)	_____
Making money	_____
Caring for or spending time with children	_____
Disciplining children	_____
Planning social events	_____
Initiating sex	_____

Pick one area from the list above and discuss how each of you can work on your own habitual behavior, thoughts, or feelings so that you live a more shared vision of male and female roles.

135

HEALTH HABIT ENERGIES

Every person has the responsibility of caring for his or her health. Before we marry, we may see caring for our bodies as a purely private matter. When we marry, our health has an impact on the marriage and all who live in our household.

The concept of "habit energies" is easily applied to health behaviors. Smoking or not smoking, eating well or not, exercising regularly or not, getting enough sleep or not—these can all be thought of as habits that affect our own health and the health of our marital relationship. Smoking, for instance, has the potential to significantly reduce the number of years a couple will spend together. We do promise "until death do us part," but hurrying death along is generally not considered part of the bargain.

It is well-known to marriage counselors that substantial weight gain over the course of a marriage puts many marriages at risk. Staying attractive to one another is a joint venture in marriage. Dealing with issues of weight and attractiveness also involves confronting habit energies that are created by the culture, such as perfect images of beauty in the media that make it difficult, especially for many women, to honor their bodies as they are. Such images also create habit energies for men and women that may make loving one beautiful, imperfect, aging spouse more difficult. If you are committed to creating a Namaste marriage in this culture, which endlessly worships the "hot" body, you will need to balance a habit of honoring your spouse's and your own body "as is" with a habit of caring for health and appearance in a responsible manner.

A bad habit never disappears miraculously; it's an undo-it-yourself project.

ABIGAIL VAN BUREN

Are the types of foods you eat and the amount of food you eat healthful? Talk with each other about the first small change you could make to improve your diet. Examples might include buying lower fat milk, having only healthy cooking oils in your kitchen, or purchasing primarily whole grain breads. How long do you think it will take to make a new habit of such small changes?

THINKING HABIT ENERGIES

One of the biggest breakthroughs in psychology in the past forty years has been the understanding that mood states and behaviors are often determined by thoughts. We become what we think. If we fill our minds with negative thoughts, we become negative people—and we feel and behave badly. If we rehearse worrisome thoughts, we fill ourselves with anxiety. In marriage, too, the way we think has a huge impact on the quality of the relationship.

The soul becomes dyed with the color of its thoughts.

MARCUS AURELIUS

Aaron Beck, one of the founders of cognitive therapy (the name for the "thoughts-drive-feelings-and-behaviors" school of psychology), has written a book about marriage titled *Love is Never Enough*. Beck's main thesis is that loving feelings do not produce loving relationships. Rather, loving feelings follow from loving behaviors, which follow from positive and undistorted thinking patterns.

Working on your thinking habit energies in marriage involves reviewing conflicts to see if your thinking made the conflict worse rather than moved it toward reconciliation. Have you ever had thoughts like these during or after a marital conflict?

- ◆ *I'm not backing down on this one.*
- ◆ *She (he) is just plain wrong!*
- ◆ *I've had enough of this nonsense!*
- ◆ *I can't believe anyone can think that way!*
- ◆ *I'll just wait until he (she) apologizes.*
- ◆ *I'm just going to give her (him) a bit of the old cold shoulder.*
- ◆ *If that's how he's (she's) going to be, I'll just quit giving sexual energy in this relationship.*
- ◆ *It's ridiculous that we have the same conflict over and over!*
- ◆ *If he (she) would change, things would be fine.*

These are only a few examples of the kinds of thoughts that can increase conflict in marriage. We all have them occasionally. Some people have a strong habit energy that produces such thoughts frequently.

⚷ Think of a recent stressor or conflict. On a page in a notebook, draw a vertical line down the center. On the left side, write down all your thoughts that were negative, inflammatory, distorted, or otherwise unhelpful in the stressful situation. In the right column, rewrite each negative thought in a healthier way. Here's an example:

NEGATIVE THOUGHT	BETTER THOUGHT
I can't believe she is this way!	*She is different from me. My task is to accept and honor her as she is.*

The practice of reviewing the unhelpful thoughts that occur in conflict situations can help you begin to notice them as they occur and cut short their negative effects.

⚷ Begin to tune into your "self-talk"—the things you say to yourself when you are under stress, when someone compliments or criticizes you, or when you make a mistake. Listen for harsh self-talk, and begin to replace it with more compassionate talk (like you might say to a friend in the same situation). It may be helpful to use a similar column approach as in the first exercise above (negative self-talk and positive self-talk).

To make a deep mental path, we must think over and over the kinds of thoughts we wish to dominate our lives.

HENRY DAVID THOREAU

🔑 Read and discuss the ideas on self-acceptance below.

SELF-ACCEPTANCE

You have probably heard a great deal about the importance of self-esteem. I prefer the slightly different concept of self-acceptance. Whereas self-esteem is about having an abiding feeling of liking ourselves, self-acceptance adds a gentle awareness that we are finite, that we have faults.

Our tendency toward either self-acceptance or self-criticism is a thinking habit energy that can determine a great deal about our level of happiness and the quality of our relationships. If you or your partner grew up in a home that was abusive or highly critical, your sense of self-acceptance still may be less than it could be. Sometimes this appears as a tendency toward depression or being hard on oneself. Other times it comes out as anger or being critical of others.

If the self-acceptance problem is pronounced and does not improve, seek counseling. Going through life without accepting yourself is like trying to swim with sandbags around your ankles. Being too hard on yourself will not allow you to develop the kind of consistent honoring interactions with your spouse that make for a rewarding personal life.

We sow our thoughts, and we reap our actions; we sow our actions, and we reap our habits; we sow our habits, and we reap our characters; we sow our characters and we reap our destiny . . .

C. A. HALL

EMOTIONAL HABIT ENERGIES

Do you have a propensity toward any negative moods that affect your marriage? Is your temper volatile? Are you often melancholy or sad? Do you spend a lot of time in needless worry? These kinds of negative emotional habit energies can drag down any marriage. Some people need help from medicines to change such emotions, but even in those cases, there is plenty of room to work on the "I" in marriage by learning about how negative thinking habits help produce or worsen negative moods.

> ⚷ Of the following three emotions, which do you experience most frequently?
>
> ◆ Sadness
> ◆ Anxiety
> ◆ Anger
>
> If you answered sadness, try a daily ritual of writing down what you are grateful for. Sadness and gratitude do not easily co-exist. For anxiety or anger, try spending five or ten minutes per day just breathing slowly and deeply while focusing on a phrase such as "peaceful and calm." This practice can help teach your body the relaxation response to stress. Your body can learn a new, more healthful habit (reacting with more calmness and less anger or anxiety). If negative emotional habit energies persist and you cannot make significant progress on your own, seek professional help. You and your marriage deserve it.

AFFECTION HABIT ENERGIES

Every home has a different way of approaching affection. Often spouses are frustrated with one another because one came from a family in which overt affection was rare, and the other came from a warm, physically-demonstrative family.

Affection is to a Namaste marriage what air is to your body. You can go without air for short stretches by holding your breath, but pretty quickly you get quite focused on getting the next breath. Affection in strong marriages isn't quite as regular as breathing, but it's almost as predictable and reliable—there every

True life is lived when tiny changes occur.

LEO TOLSTOY

day to signal that the relationship is a place of safety, warmth, and love. As we have seen in *Make connection the norm* (practice #2), the language of touch continues to be spoken fluently in a good marriage. It is the first language of love that every human infant learns if treated well by his or her parents.

If one or both of you tend to think of affection as optional or as "something I'm just not into"—or if you have developed a habit of rejecting affection because it is usually given only as a prelude to a request for sex—reconsider the importance of making daily affection a habit in your relationship.

Does affection occur easily and frequently in your marriage? If not, what can each of you work on to contribute to a steadier flow of this important love language? Begin to get clear about the kind of affection you want and change habit energies that stand in the way.

CONFLICT HABIT ENERGIES

Habit energies related to conflict have already been addressed in the chapter on *Bring honoring to conflict* (practice #3). There we discussed how some people are volatile, some validating, and some avoiding. The habit of how we respond to conflict is usually so deeply ingrained that we can spend a good portion of our marriages working to create a habit that does not tend toward either volatility or avoidance. Discussing your different approaches to conflict can keep both of you aware of the need to work on them. This is preferable to simply living out non-conscious conflict habit energies that have the power to make your marriage far less than it can be.

Be patient with everyone, but above all with yourself. I mean, do not be disheartened by your imperfections, but always rise up with fresh courage. How are we to be patient in dealing with our neighbor's faults if we are impatient in dealing with our own?

FRANCIS DE SALES

SEXUAL HABIT ENERGIES

Just as every family passes down a model of male and female roles, every family has its own approach to sexuality. Psychologists Miriam and Otto Ehrenberg have called family "the intimate circle" because family members live in close proximity daily to personal matters such as dressing or undressing, showering, and using the bathroom. In addition to such daily activities, families are the context in which boys and girls learn about affection (from the warm or cold atmosphere in the home) and about sexuality (from communication of attitudes).

According to the Ehrenbergs, authors of *The Intimate Circle*, there are four ways families approach sexuality:

Repressive: Sexuality is not talked about except in terms of morality or with warnings about its many dangers. Normal sexual thoughts, feelings, or developmental behaviors may be the object of punishment or ridicule.

Avoidant: Parents deal with sexuality by not dealing with it. Children grow up in a sexual vacuum that is filled by peers or other outside influences.

Obsessive: Children are exposed to too much sexual information and stimuli. Parents may allow young children to watch inappropriate or even pornographic movies and may fail to keep their own sexual behavior private.

Expressive: Questions about sexuality are handled as they come up in age-appropriate ways. The couple models regular affection and gives children the sense that they are still lovers. Sexual activity, however, is kept private.

For most couples, the further they get from the honeymoon, the more likely it is that family-of-origin habit energies about sexuality will affect their relationship. Certain sexual experiences inside or outside the family are also part of the history that couples may need to discuss as they move further into being vulnerable with one another in their sexual relationship.

Habit, if not resisted, soon becomes necessity.

AUGUSTINE

These might include sexual play with age-mates in childhood, sexual experiences in adolescence, or any sexual abuse or assault experiences.

Sexual habit energies can develop from your relationship with each other too. Sex can become something that is withheld when conflict is unresolved or an activity that is avoided because of too much tension about frequency or performance. These habit energies take away from the great potential of sex to be a celebration of your union. Each partner in a marriage can review his or her own sexual habit energies to determine whether they help create a loving marriage. A partner who is obsessed with sex has plenty to work on to put sex in its place alongside the many other joys in life. A partner who has little interest in sex can explore this habit energy with the goal of awakening a joyful sexuality.

Finally, some of the sexual habits that men and women bring to their marriages are developed in response to the larger culture. Women are encouraged to develop body-image conflicts by a culture obsessed with thinness. Men are raised in a culture that objectifies women and teaches men little about the emotional intimacy that is required for the best experience of sex in marriage. For both men and women, views of sexuality are shaped from an early age by television, movies, music, and other media.

It is easy to perform a good action, but not easy to acquire a settled habit of performing such actions.

ARISTOTLE

> Discuss the four types of families on page 142. Which describes your family of origin the best? Are the sexual habit energies you carry from that early part of life conducive to a beautiful sexual relationship in marriage? Discuss with each other one sexual habit energy you each feel you could work on to improve your sex life.

WORK HABIT ENERGIES

Don't trade the very stuff of your life, time, for nothing more than dollars. That's a rotten bargain.

RITA MAE BROWN

By far the most common and problematic work habit energy in our culture is workaholism—a commitment to work that leaves little time for relationships, leisure, or spirituality. The importance of living by a balance ethic instead of a work ethic has already been discussed (see page 43). Changing a workaholic habit energy requires a commitment to limiting work hours and may involve openness to working in a new setting or field. Addressing workaholism can raise important issues related to priorities, money, life goals, and the definition of success.

Living as if work is the most important part of life will not allow the creation of an extraordinary, Namaste marriage. Furthermore, psychological research indicates that the impact of workaholism on children is similar to the effect of alcoholism. Children of both kinds of parents (alcoholic and workaholic) are at risk for having problems in intimate relationships.

Some marriages struggle with the opposite problem—a partner who is under-motivated to work. This is often because the person feels hopeless about his or her potential in the work world or is trying to work in a field in which she or he has no genuine interest or passion. Having an open discussion about dreams (separate from money concerns) can often point the way to a healthier engagement with work.

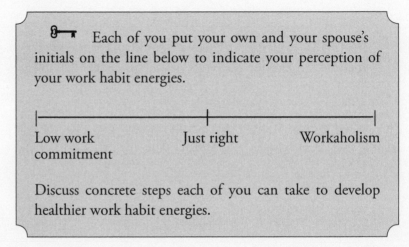

Each of you put your own and your spouse's initials on the line below to indicate your perception of your work habit energies.

|--------------------|--------------------|--------------------|

Low work   Just right   Workaholism
commitment

Discuss concrete steps each of you can take to develop healthier work habit energies.

MONEY HABIT ENERGIES

Most of us fall to one side or another on a continuum that runs from frugal to spendthrift. When both marriage partners are frugal, there are few money conflicts, but a scarcity attitude can pervade the relationship and create difficulty spending money for legitimate purposes. When both partners tend toward spendthrift, marriages can become conflicted over the pressures of mounting debt. The most difficult combination is a frugal person married to a spendthrift.

Money is a terrible master but an excellent servant.

P.T. BARNUM

When we experience our money habit energies conflicting, we owe it to our marriage to make working with these habit energies a priority. Money is a symbol for many deeper issues—freedom, power, abundance, success, and longing—so working on money habit energies can involve considerable personal and spiritual growth. Be sure to include money as part of your marital visioning meetings. Go beyond talking about it. Each of you can commit to specific, achievable behaviors that will help you work on your money habit energies and reduce conflict about money in your marriage.

⚷ Put your own and your partner's initials on the continuum below:

|————————————————|————————————————|

Frugal   Spendthrift

Discuss any concrete actions each of you can take that will help you begin to work on your own individual money habit energies. For instance, a frugal person might try tipping more generously at restaurants (or even just going to a restaurant!), and a spendthrift might commit to getting rid of credit cards if they have become a problem.

PARENTING HABIT ENERGIES

The minister at my brother's wedding kept coming back to one line: "Make new mistakes—don't make the same old mistakes your parents made!" His message was that marriage is a school of love in which we all make mistakes, but it's best to try not to make the same mistakes of past generations.

Parenting is a school of love too. All parents make mistakes despite the best of intentions. Most parents know the pull of habit energies that were formed in their own childhoods. *Why am I acting just like my mother/father when I told myself I never would?* we ask ourselves. The answer is: habit energies. Our default response to children is patterned after whatever we experienced growing up, some of which we may not want to pass on.

For many, parents are also loving models of dedication to family life. Positive habit energies that are rooted in a strong family background can serve us well, but it is still possible that these habits may clash with those of our marriage partner.

> Talk about both the good things your parents did and the mistakes they made in raising their families. If you have children, discuss whether or not you've been able to make mostly new mistakes instead of repeating the same old ones. If you do not have a family but intend to, talk about what parenting patterns you most want to avoid and how you will hold each other accountable to avoid them. Talk too about those patterns of your parents that you most want to emulate.

SPIRITUAL HABIT ENERGIES

Many people grow up with a particular faith but eventually drop it in favor of a more secular approach to life. Those who do not develop a strong, freely-chosen, adult sense of spirituality are

The path to sainthood goes through adulthood. There are no quick and easy short-cuts.

M. Scott Peck

Your children are not your children. They are sons and daughters of life's longing for itself.

Kahlil Gibran

likely to continue to see religious practice through the eyes of a child, who may have been bored by or turned off to religion or may have never been exposed to a rich religious or spiritual tradition.

Arriving at a common vision for the role of faith, prayer, spirituality and churchgoing in your marriage will involve discussion of your history of religious practice or lack thereof. How we were shaped or not shaped early in life to think of daily living as sacred impacts the choices we make about spiritual practice as adults.

Don't think that you can overcome in a day the bad habits of a lifetime . . . Be patient. Perfection will have to wait for another life, another world.

Francis de Sales

☞ Talk with each other about your experience of religion or spirituality as a child. Was it positive, exciting, meaningful, boring, maddening, or simply nonexistent? Discuss how the spiritual habit energies of your youth still affect you now. Talk about steps you can take to develop a spirituality that is more deeply integrated into your daily adult life.

☞ Make up a personal "spiritual acronym"—a word or phrase that helps you remember the key values and goals that you want to keep in your awareness on a daily basis. Here is an example, a way to help you remember and focus on the seven practices:

N: Need a shared vision (practice 1).
A: Always stay connected with my spouse (practice 2).
M: Make conflict a path to intimacy by using empathic listening (practice 3).
A: Accept and affirm my spouse "as is" (practice 4).
S: Stay focused on working on the "I" in marriage, not on changing my spouse (practice 5).
T: Treat sex as a sacred gift exchange (practice 6).
E: Extraordinary grace is hidden in the ordinary (spirituality of daily married life, practice 7).

Such an acronym provides a surprisingly useful way to begin or end your day with a five-minute review of how you want to lead your life. Busyness and stress move us away from our best selves. Even brief daily meditations on a personal spiritual acronym can function as a "reset" button for the soul.

MUTUAL MENTORING

To end this discussion of habit energies, I present what I consider a breakthrough concept for married couples: mutual mentoring. This is a way to stop the often not-so-subtle attempts of each partner to change the other. Mutual mentoring flips that dysfunctional approach on its head. Each partner picks one or more habit energies that he or she wants to change and then asks the other's help in changing them. Instead of defending against a partner who is trying to change you against your will, you decide to change certain aspects of yourself and let your partner help you with it. Usually your partner's help simply amounts to listening as you describe personal growth efforts and helping you decide what the next concrete step is for continuing with positive changes.

Here's an example of how this can work. For years I unwisely tried to persuade Claudia to use a planner to become more organized. She understandably did not take well to my attempts to change her. When, however, we began talking in terms of mutual mentoring, one of the first things she asked for my help on was learning to use a planner. Her request for help shifted the energy from me offering unsolicited help. I asked her help for my tendency to offer criticism disguised as assistance!

We all marry spouses who can help us become better people—if we will let them.

URBAN STEINMETZ

A good marriage . . . is transformative. The prevailing psychological view has been that the central dimensions of personality are fully established in childhood. But from my observations, men and women come to adulthood unfinished, and over the course of a marriage they change each other profoundly.

JUDITH WALLERSTEIN AND SANDRA BLAKESLEE

Mutual mentoring can be fit into your customary visioning meetings. Simply designate a portion of a meeting occasionally to reviewing the areas that each of you are working on. Discuss the progress (or lack thereof) on the personal growth goals each of you have chosen. Decide how to take the next step in growth. Make a commitment to your partner to do something concrete about it before your next mutual mentoring session. Mutual mentoring is a much better approach to supporting one another's efforts to change unhelpful habit energies than 1) trying to force your partner to change or 2) criticizing him or her for not changing.

To Have and to Laugh

The Powerful Lure of Habit Energies

Mr. Large Mouth Bass: Are you telling me that there are no real purple, scented worms in this pond? Then why do I keep getting hooked by those confounded things?!

Mrs. Large Mouth Bass: It's OK, honey. It's just a habit energy—albeit one that may get you filleted someday! I know those flashy silver spoon things are fake too, but I still go after them occasionally. If I keep that up, I might die with a silver spoon in my mouth!

If we keep on doin' what we always done, we'll keep on gettin' what we always got.

Barbara Lyons

<u>Key Summary Points</u>
WORK ON THE "I" IN MARRIAGE

- There is an "I" in "marriage." Working on your own physical, emotional, intellectual, social, and spiritual development will greatly benefit your marriage.
- Realize that both of you bring many good and some challenging habit energies to your marriage.
- Practice the four harbingers of happiness—affirmation in place of criticism, openness in place of defensiveness, reconnection in place of withdrawal, and honoring in place of contempt.
- Be aware of how your background affects your view of male and female roles in marriage, and be flexible as you discuss roles with your partner.
- Review your body and health habit energies. A commitment to staying healthy will likely benefit the quality and length of your marriage.
- Learn to recognize and change negative thoughts. Changing thinking habit energies that predispose you to see situations in a negative way will greatly benefit your marriage
- If you regularly experience emotional habit energies such as depression, anxiety, or anger, develop a plan to become more emotionally healthy. Seek professional help if necessary.
- Review how your sexual upbringing and history affects your sexuality today. Eliminate negative sexual habit energies that interfere with creating a beautiful sexual relationship in your marriage.
- Don't make work the focus of your life. Instead, develop a view of work that will allow you, your partner, and any children you have to thrive as whole persons.
- Work on your money habit energies to reduce the likelihood of conflict over money in your marriage.

◆ Be aware of the things your parents did well and not so well. Try at least to make new mistakes instead of the same ones your parents made.

◆ Review your spiritual and religious upbringing, and commit to concrete ways to integrate faith and spirituality into your life.

◆ Consider becoming mutual mentors for each other. Ask your partner for help in changing habit energies you want to change in yourself.

DISCUSSION QUESTIONS

1. Which of the four harbingers of happiness (affirmation, openness, reconnection, and honoring—see pages 133-134) is most challenging in your relationship? Which do you offer one another relatively regularly, and which need to be more frequent in your day-to-day interactions?

2. Is happiness a habit energy? Is it something we can directly pursue in marriage, or is it a by-product of our efforts to create loving relationships and lead good lives?

3. Our individual habit energies are shaped by cultural habit energies. The ways we think about relationships, men, women, sex, conflict, affection, work, parenting, health, and spirituality are shaped by the daily cultural messages we receive. How can you maintain an awareness that the culture may shape each of you and your relationship in a direction that is ordinary rather than extraordinary?

4. Do you think asking for a partner's help in changing one of your own habit energies would be more positive than having a partner try to change your habit energy? Do you think mutual mentoring (see page 148) could be helpful in your relationship?

The swirling, galaxy-like symbol represents the power of Make love a gift in marriage and its connection to the Creator. The flower-like image represents how sexuality blossoms in marriage when each partner focuses on making sexual loving a gift to the other. The bi-directional arrows are a reminder that the relationship between emotional and sexual intimacy in marriage flows both ways.

MAKE LOVE A GIFT

SUMMARY OF THIS PRACTICE

A strong sexual connection is important in marriage because without it married people begin to feel like roommates, business partners, co-parents, or friends who are no longer lovers. *Make love a gift* is about focusing sexuality on delighting one's partner, not on just getting one's own needs met. This way of sexual loving is inherently other-centered and sacramental.

If both of you are focused on giving the gift of your sexuality in a way that delights your partner, you'll experience the beauty of sexual love throughout your marriage.

SPIRITUAL FOCUS FOR THIS PRACTICE

What you have received as a gift, give as a gift.

Matthew 10: 8

*A*sk any marriage counselor how important sexuality is to the health of a marriage. Few couples come to counseling reporting that their sexual life is wonderful. When marriage counseling is helpful, one of the surest indicators of renewed love is a re-ignited sense of passion. The sexual life of a couple is the most obvious way that a marriage differs from other relationships. When sexuality becomes inconsistent or nonexistent (for reasons other than medical problems), a marriage quickly begins to feel like "an arrangement of convenience," a situation in which people live together after the spark is gone because it is easier than breaking up. Marriages can last this way, but such relationships do not serve as contexts for realizing the vast potential of married love.

It's usually easy for a couple to experience their relationship as highly passionate in the early stages of marriage. Such strong sexual connection in the beginning is actually rather ordinary. What is extraordinary is the ability to maintain passion through raising children and the many challenges and transitions of marriage. The fairly passionless state that marriages can settle into is quite common. Such a fate is not inevitable and usually results from the couple's difficulty processing conflicts that arise, both about the relationship in general and about sexuality in particular.

Even for couples with good communication skills, this part of marriage can become difficult because men and women generally approach sexuality in very different ways. Furthermore, every long-term marriage will have times when the sexual relationship changes, and such transitions usually cause tension. Nonetheless, it is possible, by maintaining honoring communication about these matters, to make your sexual relationship extraordinary. It is important to note that, in this context, "extraordinary" does not refer to sexual performance standards. We're not talking about getting 9.9 ratings from the male and female judges after each sexual encounter. Rather, we're talking about creating a sacramental role for sexuality in the marriage—

The world is charged with the grandeur of God.
GERARD MANLEY HOPKINS

154

one that reveals God's glory, pleasure, comfort and presence in the relationship; one that changes and grows and requires constant communication, adjustment, and willingness to learn how to love passionately at every stage of life.

We live in a culture that bombards us with messages about sexuality. Almost every issue of many women's and men's magazines has a headline which promises to reveal, at long last, the secrets of truly gratifying sex. This sells a lot of magazines, of course, and these articles occasionally contain some helpful information. The cumulative effect of these messages, however, can make it more difficult to live with the joys and tensions that are part of the reality of sex in marriage. Magazines, movies, and television give us a "highlight reel" of concepts about sex and too little information about how to communicate about it in marriage. Consequently, many people end up with distorted ideas of how sex should be in marriage or caricatured notions of male and female sexuality. Focusing on "how it's supposed to be" or wondering how it is for everyone else can take away from creating an ongoing, honoring sexuality in your own marriage.

What is lacking in secular culture is a model of sexuality grounded in a spiritual view of sex. Unfortunately, Christianity's history is not a good one when it comes to providing a positive framework for how to think about married sexuality. For too long, sexuality was presented as a short list of do's and a long list of don'ts. Being sexual was seen as less holy than being celibate, and marriage was considered the place to allow controlled expression for what were thought of as essentially sinful desires. Modern theological statements, while affirming of the dual functions of sexuality in marriage (procreation and binding the couple together in love), are not intended to provide couples with specific ideas about how to create a sacred sexual relationship.

When things don't work well in the bedroom, they don't work well in the living room either.

WILLIAM MASTERS

THE GIFT EXCHANGE MODEL

Clearly, married couples need a spirituality of sexuality that affirms the sacredness of sexual expression in marriage. They also need specific ideas about how to create a rich and rewarding sexual life. To both of these aims I offer what I call the "gift exchange" model of married sexuality. This model is based on the goal of creating an other-centered approach to sexual loving which leads to a delightful flow of energy that is similar to what we feel in a Christmas gift exchange. The Christmas metaphor is an appropriate one because sexuality is inherently spiritual and can lead to new life, both literally and in the continual rebirth of a couple's passion and love for one another.

Do you remember being a child at Christmas time, wondering how many of the items on your wish list you would get? Young children make Christmas magical, but they are generally self-centered when it comes to gifts. They want what they want, and they often create a fuss if they don't get what they want. Many adults bring a similar energy to married sexuality.

As adults we learn in time that the thrill of giving someone the perfect gift for Christmas far outweighs the enjoyment of staying focused only on getting what we want. When we receive a gift that is truly thoughtful and selected just for us, we feel a desire to reciprocate in kind. This is the kind of energy exchange that is created in Namaste marriages.

The gift exchange model requires a primary focus by each spouse on delighting her or his partner the way the partner most enjoys being delighted. In other words, don't give a gift that you want; give a gift that your partner wants! It would be nice if those gifts were one and the same, but often they are not. He might like to make love in a passionate rush; she might like to take an hour by candlelight. The gift exchange model involves each partner actively looking to help the other's dreams of beautiful sexual loving come true. This model offers a deeply spiritual approach to sexuality because it recognizes that by centering not on ourselves but on our partner, we can make God's gift of sexual loving a grace-filled experience.

The gift exchange model implies a constant ebb and flow, a focus on delighting one another in a way that is reciprocated repeatedly throughout the marriage. St. Francis of Assisi said

The manner of giving is worth more than the gift.
PIERRE CORNEILLE

that it is in giving that we receive, and this is true in married sexuality as well as in other aspects of life. Note, however, that the gift exchange model does not mean that we must always focus on our partner's desires and not our own. Nor does it mean that the receiver should be passive in the sexual encounter. Receiving a gift with enthusiasm and active participation is preferable to being passive. When the gift exchange model of sexuality is practiced regularly in marriage, giver and receiver become difficult to distinguish. This is because giving a gift to one's partner returns great pleasure and joy to the giver. Likewise, allowing oneself to be the focus of sexual delight can release the beauty of one's sexuality as pure gift to one's partner. Giving and receiving blend together when lovemaking approaches its potential to be a sacred exchange of energies. The two become one.

Happiness is a by-product of an effort to make someone else happy.

GRETTA PALMER

Nested Meditation

Make love.

Make love
a gift exchange.

Make love
a gift. Exchange
desire for delight.

Make love
a gift. Exchange
desire for delight-
ing the love of your life.

At its best, sexuality in marriage is other-centered. When each spouse focuses on understanding what the other enjoys most and offers that as a pure gift (not as a way of getting something for oneself), the relationship becomes charged with the energy of an ongoing sensual, erotic gift exchange.

PRACTICING
MAKE LOVE A GIFT
IN YOUR MARRIAGE

Perhaps you've heard the story about the group of unfortunates in Hades who are given a large kettle of soup to eat. Each is also given a spoon with a handle so long that the ravenous diners are making a complete mess of trying to feed themselves. By contrast, in heaven there's a group seated around a similar large kettle of soup, supplied with the same long-handled spoons. Everyone at this table, however, is well fed without a mess because the diners in heaven have figured out that they must use the long-handled spoons to feed the person across the table.

This is how the gift exchange model of married sexuality works. When we focus only on ourselves, we're likely to create a real mess of it. When we focus on nourishing our partner's sexuality, we can create a beautiful, marriage-long gift exchange.

Over the next fifteen pages or so, I'll offer as much insight as I can about how to navigate the sometimes confusing waters of married sexuality. Nonetheless, no book can give answers for all possible situations—and sex in marriage isn't really something that has an answer. It's simply a beautiful and sometimes challenging part of the relationship that goes best if you participate in a marriage-long discussion about it with your spouse.

THE GIFT OF RECIPROCAL ENERGIES

Women and men often differ on the emphasis they place on the interactive relationship between emotional closeness and sexual intimacy. Women generally feel that an increase in emotional closeness can lead to more frequent and satisfying sex in a mar-

You musn't force sex to do the work of love or love to do the work of sex.

MARY MCCARTHY

riage. However, for most women the emotional closeness needs to be sustained over time. The overall context of the relationship needs to feel close and honoring for most women to feel genuine sexual desire. Sweet-talking someone for an hour before an intended sexual encounter may or may not lead to the desired end in the short run. In contrast, continuously treating someone with respect and working at emotional closeness creates a context in which being sexual simply flows more easily for the majority of women.

Men, on the other hand, often complain that they would feel emotionally closer if their wives were more interested in sex. Many men feel rejected or unwanted when their wives communicate directly or indirectly that they do not want to make love as often as their husbands would prefer.

Here we have the makings of an exceedingly common marital standoff. The woman wants more passion in the marriage, but is waiting for more emotional closeness, and may feel frustrated that her husband does not seem to need or want as much of that kind of closeness. The man wants more passion in the marriage too, but he is angry and hurt that his wife does not desire him more in a physical way, and his interactions with her are therefore tinged by the strong emotional responses that result from feeling rejected.

These roles are sometimes reversed, but it is most commonly the woman who wants more emotional connection as a prerequisite to more or better sex and the man who wants more or better sex in order to feel more fully loved and accepted by his wife. The way out of this confusing maze is for both partners to realize that there is a reciprocal relationship between emotional closeness and sexual intimacy in marriage. Increased emotional closeness usually improves sexuality. Better sex leads to more emotional closeness. It is not strictly a one-way street. Both partners working on emotional and sexual intimacy throughout the marriage is most likely to result in sex being a mutually celebratory experience. This reciprocal relationship fits well with the gift exchange model. The partner who wants more frequent sex can focus on

Sex has become one of the most discussed subjects of modern times. The Victorians pretended it did not exist; the moderns pretend that nothing else exists.

FULTON J. SHEEN

giving the gift of emotional closeness. The partner who is more focused on emotional closeness can give the gift of sexual loving to help build other forms of intimacy. (Note that many people, according to marriage expert Michele Weiner-Davis, do not feel strong sexual desire until after they are sexually aroused. Waiting for desire to show up first can leave one's partner feeling hurt and unloved.)

Emotional closeness includes a sense of day-to-day connection, a trust based on honesty and fidelity, a prevailing spirit of kindness and affirmation, consistent affection, the ability to talk openly with one another, having fun together, and connecting at a spiritual level. The more of these energies that a couple develops in their marriage, the more the sexual relationship is likely to flourish.

Women complain about sex more often than men. Their gripes fall into two categories: (1) not enough, (2) too much.

ANN LANDERS

Discuss which of you is more likely to see the relationship between emotional and sexual closeness as follows:

Emotional closeness ------------------> Sexual closeness
(leads to)

Sexual closeness ---------------------> Emotional closeness
(leads to)

What would it be like to accept that the arrow points in both directions, and that each of you can offer emotional and sexual closeness as a gift to the other?

THE GIFT OF CREATING A SHARED SEXUAL VISION

Despite the openness about sexuality in our culture, most married couples continue to find it difficult to talk honestly and openly about their sexual lives. Few couples ever take the time to

Is sex important in married life? Yes, it is. It is one of the cements which holds the bricks of married life together. But the when, the how, the how often, and the quality can only be determined by the people involved.

WILLIAM LEDERER
AND DON JACKSON

actually create a shared vision for how they would like their sexual relationship to be. Often each partner has his or her own idea of how it should go, but those individual visions are usually different, and the tension between them is frequently played out in a cycle of nonverbal sexual initiatives and rejections rather than through the more direct process of open discussion.

Without a shared sexual vision, many couples spend their marriages with far more sexual frustration and misunderstanding than is necessary. Sexuality in such marriages can end up being less enjoyable, less spiritual, and less celebratory than it was created to be.

In your separate notebooks, write down and then discuss your answers to the following questions:

- Ideally, how often would we make love?
- Who should take the initiative for lovemaking?
- How much time should a typical sexual encounter take? Should the pace be slow, fast, or vary depending on the situation?
- How should we handle situations in which one of us wants to make love and the other doesn't?
- How can we keep from getting into a predictable sexual routine that introduces boredom into our lovemaking?
- How do we want to think of the role of lovemaking in our marriage? Do we see it as a sacred time of closeness to one another and to God? A time to be playful and free? A time to experience enjoyment and let go of stress?
- How often should we discuss our love life, including our sexual likes and dislikes?
- How should we deal with sexual problems that seem to be beyond our ability to resolve? Are we willing to go to counseling for such problems?

Agree to make talking about your sexuality and your sexual vision an ongoing part of marital visioning meetings.

8—▪ Read through the "Six Principles for Creating a Shared Sexual Vision" on page 164 and note the ones you think you need to discuss. Then schedule some time in a marital visioning meeting to talk about them. Sexual issues are difficult for many couples to talk about without moving toward conflict, so be sure to use empathic listening (see pages 87-95) to surface and understand one another's feelings.

THE GIFT OF ENJOYING FOUR KINDS OF TOUCH

Our bodies were created by God for sharing and enjoying four kinds of touch, all of which can be offered repeatedly as gifts throughout marriage. Some sexual problems arise from one or both members of a couple focusing too much on the fourth and not enough or not at all on the other three. The four kinds of touch are:

1. Day-to-day affection (handholding, brief hugs, snuggling);
2. Relaxing touch (massage);
3. Sensual touch (caressing or erotic touch in non-genital areas); and
4. Genital touch (full sexual contact in foreplay and intercourse).

Too much focus on genital touch can lead to sexual expression becoming mechanical, predictable, or unsatisfying. Regular practice of the other three kinds of touch is important for creating a marriage in which sexuality is expressive of the deep emotional and spiritual connection of the couple.

Most of the joy of living comes out of giving . . . without strings attached.

GARY EMERY

163

SIX PRINCIPLES FOR CREATING A SHARED SEXUAL VISION

1. **Honor male and female.** Many married people eventually fall into the trap of stereotyping their spouses ("Men—sex is all they think about!" or "Women—they just don't want it!"). These statements are an attempt to put sometimes-frustrating sexual differences in perspective, but such thoughts denigrate a partner's God-given sexuality. They fail to convey honoring for a spouse's individuality. None of us deserves to be grouped with "men" or "women." Honor male and female means spending a lifetime learning to understand the particular man or woman who is your partner and lover for life.

2. **Let your passion be unbridled.** Marriage is the place to enjoy the full sacredness and pleasure of sexuality. Create a vision that keeps your love life playful, active, adventuresome—what priest and sociologist Andrew Greeley has called "unbridled." Boredom and utter predictability, in contrast, are "bridled" and usually lead to one or both partners feeling dissatisfied. Difficulty letting go into unbridled sexuality may be related to lack of emotional intimacy, health problems, lack of a shared sexual vision, past sexual hurts (from the marriage or before), or a longstanding view that sex is a duty or is dirty. Developing an unbridled sexuality may require working through such problems, perhaps with the help of a counselor.

3. **Make sure you know the gifts your partner enjoys.** It's difficult to give a gift if you don't know what your partner wants. As you create a shared sexual vision, make sure you talk openly about the kinds of gifts each of you enjoys in lovemaking. If you'd like your partner to romance you slowly, make sure he or she knows that. If you prefer a certain approach to foreplay, make that clear. If you enjoy the ability to talk with each other during lovemaking (instead of silence), let your partner know. When you are aware of the gifts your partner enjoys receiving, follow through. Remember: give the gift your partner wants, not the gift you want, and be sure you respect what your partner does *not* like.

4. **Balance "less is more" and "more is more."** Most marriages have one partner who desires sex more frequently (more is more) and another who wants it less frequently (less is more). This difference causes chronic tension in numerous marriages. A spiritual way to handle this common problem is for the "more is more" spouse to work on giving the gift of space (avoiding pressuring for sex) and the "less is more" partner to work on giving the gift of sexual initiative. It's also important to learn to say no to sex in a way that does not de-eroticize the relationship over time. Saying, "Not now, but I'd love to make love with you this weekend" has a different effect than just turning away or saying "Not now."

5. **Honor the "slow hand" and the "heated rush."** It's common for spouses to have different ideas about the pace of lovemaking. In creating your sexual vision, talk about how you can gift each other by honoring your partner's preferred pace. Always following the same pace may leave one partner feeling like her or his sexuality is not being honored.

6. **Base your passion on honesty.** Don't fake pleasure. Talk honestly about what you enjoy or don't enjoy. Talk openly too about how to stay attractive to each other—keeping your bodies healthy and in shape. Use empathic listening (see pages 87-95) to talk about sexual matters that seem especially sensitive or difficult.

We have already addressed the role of day-to-day affection in making connection the norm in marriage (see pages 59-61). It bears repeating here that it is important that affection flow freely in your relationship. If it only flows when you want sex, you will end up with a partner who rejects both your affectionate and your sexual initiatives. I advise couples to make sure there are at least ten affectionate interactions for every sexual one.

Massage is a form of touch that many couples share early in their relationship but enjoy less frequently over time. Massage is a wonderful way to practice the gift exchange model. Because its intent is to relax one's stressed, weary or aching partner, not to get something for oneself, massage is inherently other-centered. In a busy, stressful world, exchanging massages brings an oasis of calm and relaxation into a marriage. Massage can become confusing or may even be avoided by some if it is always linked to an initiative for sexual activity. It can certainly serve as a prelude to lovemaking, but massage works best to build up your love if that is not always the case.

Sensual touch is called sensate focus by sexuality experts. Sensual touch focuses on light caress of areas other than those normally considered most erogenous. The concept is to expand a couple's idea of their sexuality by encouraging exploration of the God-given delights of the entire human body. This is particularly helpful to couples who have developed performance anxiety in their lovemaking. Performance anxiety refers to fears about one's ability to please one's partner sexually or to "perform" adequately. This kind of anxiety can cause avoidance of lovemaking, tuning out during the experience, or attempting to rush through it before anything goes wrong. Sensual touch frees couples to take the focus off genital touch and learn to enjoy one another's entire body. This kind of touching in marriage is sacred and prayerful, because it involves focusing on what is enjoyable for one's partner without pressuring or hurrying toward intercourse.

In marital therapy, non-genital sensual touch is often recommended with a "proscription of intercourse." This means that couples spend time in sensual touch without progressing to

When this evening comes, lie down in each others' arms. Let the day slip away. And enjoy the heaven of the moment.

WILLIAM MARTIN

There is nothing in the whole realm of sexual expertise so effective as these three little sentences: "Honey, I really want to love you, and I want to make you feel loved. But I don't know how. Can you help me?"

Urban Steinmetz

intercourse. This may seem unnatural to some, but agreeing in advance that the goal is not to have intercourse can free the couple to develop an awareness of the whole-body nature of sexuality. Giving each other "non-demand" sensual touch can awaken couples to the power of the other-centered, gift exchange model.

This book is not intended as a guide to foreplay or love-making in marriage, and I will therefore not attempt to provide instruction on genital touch. While there are many secular materials offered on this topic, there is no better instruction available than what you can learn from your marriage partner if you cultivate an ongoing, honest discussion of sexuality. The openness and vulnerability that such communication requires can deepen the marriage bond.

1. Discuss how daily affection impacts the quality of your sexual life. Have affection and sexuality become too closely connected, such that one of you sometimes rejects affection because it is only given when sex is desired? Talk about what the best ratio of affectionate and fully sexual encounters should be in your marriage.

2. Discuss massage and how often you might enjoy giving one another whole body massages, foot rubs, head rubs, and so on. Then follow through.

3. Spend time caressing one another by candlelight with no intent of proceeding to intercourse. Avoid touching the most erogenous areas so that you can explore how the entire body has been wired by our Maker for sensual delight. Practice communicating during this sensate focus exercise about what feels good, what to do more of and less of, and expressing appreciation for the gift of sensual caress.

4. Finally, talk openly about the kind of genital touch that makes you most ready for wonderful lovemaking. This is not a time to be vague. Talk, too, about intercourse itself. What makes it most beautiful and enjoyable for you? What detracts from the experience? Being open and vulnerable about these matters can create a deeper level of emotional trust and intimacy between you.

THE GIFT OF
COMMUNICATING ABOUT SEXUAL PROBLEMS

The late Urban Steinmetz, author of a delightful exploration of marriage titled, *Strangers, Lovers, Friends* had a simple rule for communicating about sexuality in marriage: "Talk when it's fun, really talk when it's not." Sexuality is relatively easy to talk about when it's going well. Many couples make the mistake of not communicating about sexuality when it is going through more difficult times. Some get so used to sex being problematic that they cease any serious exploration of how to improve this part of their marriage. This lack of communication is often because the partners feel it is no longer worthwhile to create tension over something that has been discussed repeatedly but continues to be a problem. Much like an injured joint can become frozen if a person avoids moving it for fear of pain, a couple's sexuality can lock up in unsatisfying patterns when a couple stops talking about it.

Many married couples live with mild or serious sexual problems without ever finding a way to improve this part of their relationship. Typically, they make some attempts to address the problems but find that sexual issues can be quite difficult to discuss openly and gently without hurting feelings. Therefore, many people eventually avoid talking about sexual problems altogether. This lack of communication about sexual problems is, in fact, why enduring passion is beyond the ordinary—because relatively few couples discuss their sexual issues openly enough or frequently enough to avoid getting caught in unsatisfying patterns.

Unresolved sexual issues affect the entire marriage and place some marriages at risk for affairs and the hurtful fallout they create. While this book is not a sex therapy manual, it is useful to review some of the common problems that create tension in married couples' sexuality. These include (but are not limited to) those listed in the box on page 169.

This partial list of potential sexual problems in marriage could make sexuality look like a minefield. Working through

Acting is not very hard. The most important things are to be able to laugh and cry. If I have to cry, I think of my sex life. And if I have to laugh, well, I think of my sex life.

GLENDA JACKSON

Let there be spaces in your togetherness.

KAHLIL GIBRAN

such problems can be challenging, but doing so is part of what keeps a committed couple communicating at a deep level. For most couples, making progress on such issues will require all of the communication skills covered in *Bring honoring to conflict* (practice #3). Empathic listening is especially important in addressing sexual difficulties because of the special vulnerability that human beings feel when talking about sexual matters with one another.

Most couples will benefit greatly from simply maintaining an accepting attitude toward sexual problems. Railing against having problems and assuming that your sex life should be problem-free is a sure way to magnify them. Accepting that sexual tension between married people is common allows a couple to take a long-term, honoring perspective on working through problems.

Sometimes a couple finds it difficult to make progress with sexual matters on their own. Such couples can benefit from time with a qualified counselor. Be sure to work with someone who will actually challenge you to risk trying more effective ways to relate to one another emotionally and physically instead of just letting you talk endlessly about your problems.

⚷ Review the list of sexual problems on page 169. Write down those that apply to your relationship. Plan a marital visioning meeting to review these problems in an honoring way and to make a plan to improve them. Agree that your sexual relationship is worth the time, energy, and patience necessary to improve it. Discuss whether your sexual relationship is worth the time and expense of professional counseling if you cannot improve things on your own.

COMMON SEXUAL PROBLEMS IN MARRIAGE

1. Feeling pressured to have sex too often.
2. Feeling upset that sex is not frequent enough.
3. Lack of interest in sex or strong aversion to sex.
4. Dissatisfaction with regular sexual routine.
5. Lack of sexual satisfaction (for example, orgasm problems).
6. Difficulty getting or maintaining an erection sufficient for intercourse.
7. Premature ejaculation—completion of male arousal cycle before one or both partners desire.
8. Anxiety about performance problems.
9. Feeling like a failure—unable to please partner.
10. Not feeling attracted as much to one's partner anymore (may be related to health, weight, or aging issues).
11. Not comfortable with own body image or attractiveness.
12. Dissatisfaction with restrained nature of lovemaking.
13. Feeling like affection is given only as prelude to sex.
14. Being bothered by a partner's attention to or attention from other people.
15. Past hurtful sexual experiences (in marriage or before, including sexual abuse as a child or rape).
16. Negative or guilty attitudes about sexual pleasure from family of origin or other sources.
17. Hurt over repeatedly being turned down sexually by partner.
18. Feeling partner is more focused on work or children than on the couple's relationship (including sexuality).
19. Fatigue or health problems (for example, pain during intercourse) as reason given to not make love.
20. Hurt or confusion over a partner's masturbation or use of pornography.
21. Difficulty being sexually open or interested again after a partner's affair.
22. Seeing a partner as the mother or father of your children more than your lover (a de-eroticized view of one's partner).
23. Lack of emotional or spiritual connection making sexual activity seem shallow or unfulfilling.
24. Disagreement about openness to conceiving children; struggles with infertility.
25. Mismatch of desire related to gender differences or hormonal changes associated with menopause or aging.

THE GIFT OF COMMUNICATING ABOUT SEXUAL RHYTHMS

As with all sacred experiences, sexuality is not at its best when it feels pressured, either in terms of frequency or performance. Acknowledging that both individuals and the marriage have sexual rhythms can help create an honoring tone for sexuality that avoids forcing or pressuring sexual expression.

What are some of the sexual rhythms partners can learn to flow with in marriage? I will discuss five: weekday/weekend rhythms, the monthly rhythm, the parenting rhythm, the rhythm of good times and bad, and life cycle rhythms.

WEEKDAY/WEEKEND RHYTHMS

Some individuals prefer to be sexual spontaneously regardless of the day of the week. Others find themselves too distracted during the workweek to take time to really relax with sexuality. The important thing is to attempt to arrive at a shared vision regarding when sexuality will be considered a high priority and when it may be better to give it a rest.

THE MONTHLY RHYTHM

The awareness that their sexual behavior is connected to the awesome potential and privilege of co-creating new life (with each other and with God) is a constant reminder to married partners of the sacredness of their sexuality. In being sexual, spouses place themselves in the creative energy stream of life itself. What could be more sacred!

Honoring the monthly rhythm means realizing that the ancient cycle of fertility is an important part of married sexuality in both a spiritual and practical way. At the spiritual level, it is a reminder of the miracle of life, of how close women and men are to the Divine energy that creates life. At a more practical level, nature may have an influence on a woman's interest in and receptivity to sexuality at various times of the monthly cycle. Some women feel little variation; others feel most interested around the

In sex, trying to keep up with the Joneses is the road to disaster. To decide where sex fits into their particular marriage, a couple must look inward at the marriage, not outward at the deceptive advice and make-believe standards set by others.

WILLIAM LEDERER
AND DON JACKSON

time of ovulation, when conception is most likely. Most women prefer to avoid intercourse during menses, though some do not mind making love at this time of the month. Each couple needs to communicate openly about how the monthly cycle affects their sex life. Doing so can create a sense of keeping in sync with an ancient rhythm of human existence: the ongoing preparation of life to create new life. Even when a couple has no immediate intention of conceiving, a reverence for this cycle of life can keep alive the sense of the miraculous embedded in the everyday that is as close as our own fertility.

Couples who use natural family planning (NFP) are particularly attuned to this cycle. This involves more than just monitoring for signs of ovulation. It also involves discussion of how the cycle affects sexual desire and how the couple will adjust to the abstaining from intercourse required in "phase two" of the cycle.

THE PARENTING RHYTHM

One of the most robust findings in research on sexuality is that sexual satisfaction in marriage declines sharply after the arrival of the first child and recovers somewhat when the nest is empty. This does not mean that the decline of sexuality during the child-raising years is inevitable. Rather, it highlights the importance of continuing to communicate regularly about sexuality, making sure that the passion that created the children is not lost by exclusive focus on them. In other words, we ought not kill the goose that laid the golden eggs! Remember: A strong marriage relationship is at the heart of any highly functioning family, and a mutually satisfying sexual connection is key to having a strong marriage.

Adjusting to the rhythm of parenting requires couples to learn to "switch gears" from focus on children to focus on one another. Keeping a marriage passionate during the parenting years involves learning to draw boundaries around couple time, protecting the space necessary for emotional intimacy and sexual expression. A couple who learns to see sexuality as a form of

In this [marriage] relationship, the primary sex organ in both the man and woman is located squarely between the eyes.

URBAN STEINMETZ

171

The greatest contrast between happily married and divorcing couples may well be in the domain of sex. By the time people file for divorce, sexual deprivation of many years standing is shockingly common.

JUDITH WALLERSTEIN
AND SANDRA BLAKESLEE

prayer and a sacred way of honoring and giving to one another throughout marriage will find ways to prioritize continuing to be passionate lovers throughout the parenting years.

Depending on their roles in the marriage, men and women may experience the effects of parenting on sexuality differently. It is not unusual for a man to feel threatened by his wife's emotional intimacy with their children (especially early in the parenting years), particularly if he feels it takes away too much time and energy from her time with him. It is common for a man to allow his wife's motherhood role to affect his erotic feelings toward her. Respecting that she can be a wonderful mother, a friend, and a lover means not reducing her mentally to one or two of these roles.

Likewise, while nature is telling them to tend to the child or children they already have (and sometimes wearing them out in the process with, for example, multiple nighttime breastfeeding sessions), some mothers do not place lovemaking high on their list of priorities. Honoring in this context means remembering that sexuality is key to a strong marriage, even at times when busyness and fatigue make it easy to set aside or ignore.

THE RHYTHM OF GOOD TIMES AND BAD

Most couples still promise on their wedding days to be true to one another in good times and in bad. This applies to sexuality as well as to other parts of the marriage. If the norm in a marriage is an ongoing effort to create a passionate relationship, the couple eventually comes to believe more and more in their ability to weather the effects that external problems or marriage stresses can have on sexuality. An extraordinary, Namaste marriage can go through difficult sexual times like any marriage. What differentiates such a marriage from others is the refusal to become stuck indefinitely in negative relationship patterns or sexual problems. Couples in Namaste marriages strive to keep the dream of passion alive during difficult times. In fact, the desire to experience the beauty of sexual harmony again is a powerful motivator in such marriages for persevering through the personal growth necessary to deal with hard times.

I will be true to you in good times and in bad . . .

TRADITIONAL MARRIAGE VOW

LIFE CYCLE RHYTHMS

Finally, honoring life cycle rhythms means continuing to communicate regularly about sexuality as age-related factors such as changing hormone levels (in husband or wife), menopause, changes in body appearance or image, and changes in health status affect a couple's sexual relationship.

Maintaining a passionate relationship over the whole course of a marriage involves continually redefining passion. Couples who experience passion after many years together often describe it as somewhat less athletic and considerably more intimate than in their younger years. Passionate spouses are like nature-lovers on a fifty, sixty, or seventy-year hike. They are less inclined to look back and yearn for the beautiful scenery behind them than they are to enjoy whatever beauty is in front of them in the present moment.

To know how to grow old is the master work of wisdom, and one of the most difficult chapters in the great art of living.

HENRI FREDERIC AMIEL

Discuss the five sexual rhythms presented in this section (weekday/weekend, monthly, parenting, good times and bad, and life cycle rhythms). Which currently affect your sexuality? Spend time in empathic listening to better understand your partner's experience of these rhythms.

To Have and to Laugh

Same Marriage Bed, Different Worlds

Counselor: "Mr. And Mrs. Smith, how often do you make love?"

They reply simultaneously:

Mr. Smith: "Hardly ever, about twice a week."

Mrs. Smith: "All the time, about twice a week."

Key Summary Points
MAKE LOVE A GIFT

- Practice the other-centered, gift exchange model of sexual loving. Focus on helping your partner's dream of a passionate marriage come true.

- Realize that your sex life and your emotional intimacy are reciprocally related. Keeping a passionate connection requires continuing to find ways to be emotionally connected. Being emotionally connected requires continual efforts to create a mutually satisfying sex life.

- Make creating a shared vision for your sexuality part of your overall marital vision. In doing so, remember six important guidelines: 1) honor male and female, 2) unbridle your passion, 3) know the gifts your partner enjoys, 4) balance "less is more" and "more is more," 5) honor the slow hand and the heated rush, and 6) base your passion on honesty.

- Think of sexuality in broader terms than foreplay and intercourse. Sharing regular affection, massage, and non-genital sensual touch will help keep passion strong in your marriage.

- Assume that sexual tensions and problems will arise and learn to talk about them openly as often as is necessary.
- Talk about the various life rhythms that affect your sexual relationship, including weekday/weekend, monthly, parenting, good times and bad, and life cycle rhythms.

DISCUSSION QUESTIONS

1. Does the gift exchange model seem workable to you? That is, can both marriage partners really stay focused on helping realize the other person's dream of good sexual loving? In what ways could this approach break down in a marriage?

2. Do you agree that the relationship between emotional and sexual intimacy goes both ways? Or are you more likely to see the relationship as one-directional (for example, emotional intimacy leads to sexual intimacy)? How can your marriage avoid the standoff that occurs in many marriages—one waiting for more emotional connection to have better sex, the other waiting for better sex to have more emotional connection?

3. Do you think any married couple is perfectly matched on the matter of sexual frequency? Is the gift exchange approach to this problem (the low frequency partner trying to give the gift of more sexual encounters and the high frequency partner trying to give the gift of more affectionate-but-not-sexual encounters) the best way to bridge the gap? What about when partners' preferred sexual frequencies are much further apart?

4. Sexual problems occur in every marriage—sometimes short-term, sometimes chronic. Does knowing that sexual problems or tensions are common make it easier to consider discussing them?

The zigzag path to the sun represents the couple's sacred journey together through life toward God (Walk the sacred path). The hands in the prayer position at the top are comprised of one female and one male hand, symbolizing the importance of shared prayer and spirituality in marriage.

WALK THE SACRED PATH

SUMMARY OF THIS PRACTICE

When we say marriage is sacramental, we don't just mean that it is a sacred ritual that occurs on the wedding day. We mean, rather, that married living and loving continually reveal God's presence in our daily lives. When viewed this way, creating a Namaste marriage can be a primary way that men and women integrate faith and spirituality into their everyday lives. *Walk the sacred path* means seeing Divinity in disguise in your daily life, giving voice to that God awareness, ritualizing it in repeatable behaviors that build up your love, and responding by serving God in your home and in the world. If you see your daily married life as sacred and find ways to remind each other of this often, you will experience it to be so.

SPIRITUAL FOCUS
FOR THIS PRACTICE

Pray without ceasing.

1 Thessalonians 5:17

The spiritual focus phrase for this chapter—"Pray without ceasing"—puzzles many people. Does this mean we need to be on our knees or reciting formal prayers all day long? When we expand our definition of prayer, however, St. Paul's phrase makes more sense. Prayer is a way of pausing to acknowledge or reflect on the wonderfully mysterious, graced nature of our lives. It can also be a calling out to God for help in difficult times, which reminds us of our limits, our need for the Infinite One.

Prayer happens any time we're tuned into the sacred, and marriage is teeming with sacred moments—both joyful and difficult—if we remain attentive for them. When defined in this broad way, prayer is a two-way communication. Sometimes we call out to God in need and learn to see God responding to us in our difficulties, often through the loving support of people in our lives. Other times God communicates to us first, usually in the simple joys of life. In response, we give voice to and act upon our awareness of God's immanence by how we express love at home and in the world.

That word "immanence" is important. It means "existing within" or "extending to all parts of the created world." This is a way of thinking about God's presence that fits marriage. God is soaked through, dwelling within, everpresent in daily life—in a word, immanent. This awareness changes everything. It's as if we put on a new set of glasses and look at marriage in a different light. These spiritual glasses are not rose-colored. They simply help us see and celebrate that our lives, our concerns, our relationships are all God-colored.

Let's pause here, because all this talk about God and the spirituality of marriage can get kind of fuzzy for some people. We know we're talking about God when words just can't seem to capture what we're trying to express. We end up, like Jesus, turning to stories and metaphors to communicate about the ineffable. In the box on page 180 I offer four images. Perhaps one of them

There are within theology two lengthy and opposing traditions . . . one the doctrine of Emmanence, which holds that grace emanates down from an eternal God ... the other the doctrine of Immanence, which holds that grace immanates out from the God within the center of [our] being.

M. SCOTT PECK

will stay with you as a way to think about the spirituality of married life. Better yet, create your own image or story that says it best for you.

Though it can be challenging to put into words, spirituality in marriage is really not that complicated. It boils down to this: God is not a distant figure that lives somewhere separate from our routine existence; rather, God is alive and present in the details of our lives—most especially in our efforts to create deeply loving relationships.

Throughout this book we've already been taking a spiritual view of marriage—embracing the idea that our efforts to love each other have something to do with God and spirituality. Each of the six practices covered so far represents a part of the spiritual path of marriage. They are not simply techniques for having a good marriage but forms of spiritual practice to which we return over an over in our efforts to make our marriages the best they can be. This chapter will present some additional ideas about spirituality in marriage, but let's review first how each of the other six practices is spiritual at its core.

Create a shared vision is a spiritual practice because it builds your marriage on the solid foundation of meeting regularly to dream together and to intentionally make your marriage extraordinary. *Make connection the norm* is the spiritual practice of ensuring that regular affection, kindness, and heart-to-heart communication keep your marriage close. *Bring honoring to conflict* is a way to practice "love is patient, love is kind" by stopping hurtful interactions, reconnecting, apologizing, listening deeply, and solving problems. *Give up the search for the perfect lover* is the spiritual practice of acceptance—the offering of unconditional love to your partner (which none of us can ever do perfectly!). *Work on the "I" in marriage* represents your individual commitment to continual personal and spiritual growth, which in time allows your marriage to blossom. *Make love a gift* is the spiritual practice of sexuality in marriage in an other-centered way which recognizes that the creative, loving energy of God is present when you make love.

The winds of grace are always blowing but it is you who must raise your sails.

RABINDRANATH TAGORE

Awe enables us to perceive in the world intimations of the divine, to sense in small things the beginning of infinite significance, to sense the ultimate in the common and the simple; to feel in the rush of the passing the stillness of the eternal.

ABRAHAM JOSHUA HESCHEL

FOUR IMAGES FOR FINDING GOD BENEATH THE ORDINARY IN MARRIAGE

IMAGE #1: SALAMANDERS UNDER ROCKS

When our family visited the Great Smoky Mountains several years ago, our six-year-old daughter Elisabeth hunted for salamanders for hours beneath the rocks at the edge of the stream by which we were camped. I can still hear her voice ring out with the joy of discovery: "I found another one!" That's how God's presence is uncovered in marriage. When a couple is always looking for the grace there is to be found hidden beneath the surface of things, they find it with surprising regularity. We invite into our lives that to which we give our abiding attention.

IMAGE #2: RHUBARB PIE

The rhubarb pie I'm so fond of would be good without grated orange peel, but it is *superb* with it! Spirituality is the grated orange peel of marriage! It is the extra something that makes a good marriage truly extraordinary, the ingredient that allows a couple to experience the transcendent dimensions of love between human beings and between the Creator and the created. As married people, we taste and see the goodness of God in the simplest of every-day experiences, including all of our efforts to grow in our understanding of genuine love.

IMAGE #3: A RIVER OF GRACE

Taking the "Maiden of the Mist" boat ride beneath Niagara Falls made me feel like I was looking up at the mouth of God pouring out infinite love in every instant of existence. For me, the Niagara River falling so steadily and beautifully symbolizes the amazing source of energy that is available to married couples. Grace flows constantly into our lives in the guise of everyday joys and challenges.

IMAGE #4: A BILLBOARD

Maybe you've seen the billboard I passed recently along the highway. It read: *Loved the wedding! Now invite me to the marriage. – God*

How do you invite God to be part of your marriage? By recognizing that God is already there in every moment of married love. Dan Zak—a pastor and friend—refers to the "sacra-ment of the moment." By this he means that God is revealed to us in any moment to which we are fully present—not consumed by regret for the past or anxiety about the future. Giving your abiding attention to the ordinary events of daily living and loving and remaining open to the grace that flows in them—this is the most basic way to invite God to your marriage.

Remembering that each of the practices is a form of spiritual discipline helps us recall that marriage is much deeper than it appears. Learning to love well in marriage is a beautiful and difficult process that requires of us a willingness to grow spiritually.

Many people think of spirituality as something that occurs primarily for an hour or so per week at church or only in structured prayers. This final chapter of *The Seven Spiritual Practices of Marriage* presents a more integrated way to think of and experience the spiritual dimensions of married life. Karl Rahner, the great twentieth-century Jesuit theologian, spoke about the *liturgy of the world.* His idea was that all of life is graced. Every day-to-day experience is potentially revealing of God. We all live in this ongoing liturgy of the world, but we don't always remember that daily life is sacred. We get bored, stressed, tired, and distracted. Many people go to church hoping to find a God they cannot seem to find in daily life. In reality, our experience of the *liturgy of the Word* (church) is greatly enhanced by our participation in the liturgy of the world. Church communities are enlivened when their members know a deep and daily experience of God and assemble to celebrate God's abundant grace.

Recall the two meanings of extraordinary from the introductory chapter: going beyond and beneath the ordinary. All seven practices involve going beyond and beneath, but *Walk the sacred path* focuses more on looking beneath the ordinary than any of the others. We'll discuss:

1) seeing Divinity in disguise,
2) giving voice to God awareness,
3) ritualizing God awareness, and
4) serving from God awareness.

Whether your wedding was yesterday or fifty years ago, these four ways of practicing *Walk the sacred path* will invite God into every day of your marriage.

Earth's crammed with heaven, and every common bush afire with God.

ELIZABETH BARRETT BROWNING

The moment one gives close attention to anything, even a blade of grass, it becomes a mysterious, awesome, indescribably magnificent world in itself.

HENRY MILLER

Nested Meditation

Joy is succulent, wild!

Joy is succulent, wild
black raspberries.

Joy is succulent, wild
black raspberries
overhanging every path.

Joy is succulent, wild
black raspberries
overhanging every path,
scratching for your attention right and left.

Joy is succulent, wild
black raspberries
overhanging every path,
scratching for your attention, right? And left
mostly unpicked?

The potential for joy overhangs the path of every marriage like berries waiting to be picked. So why do we leave joy mostly unpicked? Could it be because we do not make looking for the sacred and joyful in life the focus of our daily attention? When we do, marriage is ripe with spiritual depth and companionship.

PRACTICING
WALK THE SACRED PATH
IN YOUR MARRIAGE

SEEING DIVINITY IN DISGUISE

Ralph Waldo Emerson was the originator of the phrase "Divinity in disguise." In three words, Emerson captured the essence of everyday spirituality—looking for God disguised in all people, events, and aspects of creation. Emerson's idea reminds me of how, as a child, I looked for the hidden pictures—a shoe, a hat, a rabbit—cleverly concealed in the drawing in every issue of *Highlights* magazine. As adults, we know this form of spiritual awareness from what the mystics have taught—that God is present in all things at all times.

Are you old enough to remember the hamburger ad that featured an elderly woman pulling the top bun off a burger and exclaiming, "Where's the beef?" Even though we are surrounded by God's presence at every moment, we can become so habituated to the wonders of creation or so caught up in our secular culture, that we are prone to stumble through life wondering, "Where's the sacred?"

Jesus encouraged us to look for the Divine in the ordinary. The images he used to teach about spiritual matters were drawn from everyday life. A mustard seed, a coin, a fig tree, a lamp, a bushel basket—these and many other common objects were an important part of his awareness of God. Divine presence, he taught, is in all people: the lowly, the downtrodden, and any group that gathers in his name. He also found God's love mirrored in intimate human relationships, such as the love of a woman and man or the love of a parent for a child.

A Namaste marriage is made up of two people who develop this ability to find God's presence in the world around them and

God is spreading grace around in the world like a five-year-old spreads peanut butter: thickly, sloppily, eagerly.

DONNA SCHAPER

You pray in your distress and in your need; would that you might pray also in the fullness of your joy and in your days of abundance.

KAHLIL GIBRAN

183

in their relationship. The cultivation of this awareness not only fosters each individual's spiritual growth but allows the marriage to thrive at a much deeper level than is ordinarily the case.

Victor Hugo, in *Les Miserables,* wrote that "to love another person is to see the face of God." The next two sections present two more ways of thinking about seeing Divinity in disguise in marriage.

Seeing Divinity in Disguise
REMEMBER THAT JOY MEANS GOD IS PRESENT

Pierre Teilhard de Chardin, the French Jesuit theologian and paleontologist, wrote, "Joy is an infallible sign of the presence of God." We could take issue with this, knowing that people find immoral ways to seek pleasure, but true joy is deeper than momentary pleasure. Joy is evoked by connection with, not desecration of, the sacred.

Simple joys are holy.
FRANCIS OF ASSISI

When you begin to recognize God's presence in the joy of watching a child walk for the first time, in the laughter around the dinner table, in your love of a particular hobby, in moments of deep and delicious relaxation, God is no longer a distant, up-in-the-skies figure, but an immanent and gracious river of grace flowing at every moment beneath the surface of life.

Where there is great love there are always miracles.
WILLA CATHER

Did you ever lose something and search all through the house for it and then find it right under your nose? That's how we are with God much of the time, and our marriages suffer for it. We are too much in pursuit of "happiness" while God goes unnoticed in the simple joys of life. Our conditioned desire to want more than we currently have can blind us to the riches that are hidden beneath our daily experiences. Joy isn't something we need to pursue. It's more like a deep well from which we are free to draw whenever we choose.

> 🗝 Talk with each other about what "lights you up." What makes you feel passionate about life—alive, interested, wanting to learn and experience all you can? Discuss how these aspects of your own joy are reminders of God's presence breaking through in your thoughts, emotions, and activities.

Seeing Divinity in Disguise

UNMASK GOD IN HARD TIMES

Every couple marries with the hope of sharing many joyful years together. Yet every marriage goes through hard times. The worse in "for better and worse" can come from within the relationship (communication difficulties, sexual problems) or from factors outside of the relationship (losing a job, health problems, loss of loved ones).

In a spiritually intimate marriage, both partners grow in their ability to unmask hard times, to see them as God's call to growth rather than failure or random misfortune. (Note, however, that some hardships—such as ongoing emotional or physical abuse—are certainly not a call for the victim to simply accept the situation as suffering necessary for growth.)

Urban Steinmetz, in *Strangers, Lovers, Friends,* wrote that marriages pass from the time of illusion, to the time of disillusion, to the time of misery, to the time of genuine love. Steinmetz's use of the word "misery" is strong—but the word literally means "a serious lack of contentment or happiness." Steinmetz wrote that only by persevering in our efforts to learn about love through our most difficult times do we arrive at genuine love—a marriage tested in fire and based on real experience rather than illusion, a love that knows the healing power of forgiveness.

The world breaks everyone and afterward many are strong at the broken places.
ERNEST HEMINGWAY

God is in the passage through difficult times to genuine love. It can help simply to remember and remind one another of this. The paschal mystery is a central tenet of Christianity: Life brings hardship to all, but new life and joy follow suffering.

> ✎ Write down three periods in your married or single life that could be considered "hard times." Looking back, can you see God's presence in those times? Can you see any gifts that came from the difficulties you went through?

GIVING VOICE TO GOD AWARENESS

In the prior section we focused on seeing God in the everyday. In marriage, spiritual intimacy is enhanced when we go a step further and talk about our awareness of God with each other. This is what people do, for instance, when they attend a big sporting event. First they go to the game and experience it as it happens. The next day they talk about the game with whomever will engage the discussion: "Did you see how high he leapt to catch that pass in the back of the end zone? Amazing!"

Likewise, in a spiritually close marriage, we first experience God in daily life, then we talk about it, hopefully with a level of enthusiasm similar to sports fans. "Wow, wasn't the sunshine and the cool breeze this morning great? What a gift!" Or perhaps, "Look at the variety of food we are enjoying tonight—we are so blessed!" Calling attention to our God awareness—speaking it out loud—helps us see beneath the ordinary.

Sharing traditional prayers together on a regular basis is a way of voicing God awareness. Some couples find that praying to God spontaneously out loud while in each other's presence allows them to address difficult matters and invite God's help. This sounds something like, "Dear God, be with us, help us with these money tensions that cause such conflict between us. Help each of us develop a better attitude toward money and respect the other's concerns. Help us forgive one another for our angry words and return to closeness." Priest and sociologist Andrew Greeley, in *Faithful Attraction,* presents intriguing research that couples who regularly pray together have more frequent and satisfying sex. Spiritual closeness, like emotional closeness, is related

There are only two ways to live your life. One is as though nothing is a miracle. The other is as though everything is a miracle.

ALBERT EINSTEIN

Life is this simple: We are living in a world that is absolutely transparent and the Divine is shining through it all the time. This is not just a story or a fable. It is true.

THOMAS MERTON

to the quality of a couple's physical intimacy.

Keeping in mind our broad definition of "pray always," the next three sections present three additional ways to think about giving voice to God awareness in marriage.

<u>Giving Voice to God Awareness</u>
CONSIDER "I LOVE YOU" A PRAYER AND SAY IT OFTEN

In a scene from *Fiddler on the Roof,* Tevye sings repeatedly to his wife Golda, "Do you love me?" She keeps responding with answers such as, "For twenty-five years I do your laundry and mend your socks—and you're asking if I love you?" Finally, when she relents and says, "I suppose I do," he replies, "After twenty-five years, it's nice to know."

Individuals' expectations differ on how often to say "I love you" to a marriage partner. Twenty-five years would be considered a bit of a dry spell by almost anyone! Some people believe saying it too often cheapens the phrase. Many who are not comfortable saying "I love you" daily may think that the phrase means, "Right now I am feeling in love with you." However, as a prayer, "I love you" can mean far more than expressing a feeling of love. It can even be used when the feeling of love is not prominent. "I love you" can mean "I am committed to loving you" or "I choose to love you even now when we are struggling."

When two people relate to each other authentically and humanly, God is the electricity that surges between them.

MARTIN BUBER

Others who are reluctant to say "I love you" may feel that love is better expressed in actions than in words. These people live by a "words are cheap" guideline. Often, however, they have loved ones who wish to hear the words "I love you" more regularly. Every counselor has worked with people who have said, "I know my parents loved me, but it would have been helpful to hear them say it."

Whether or not you come to think of "I love you" as a prayer, it is important to clarify the norm in your relationship for how often those words will be said. I think saying them daily is healthy and prevents couples from going long periods without putting into words their commitment to love one another.

> ⚷ Discuss how often you want to say "I love you" in your marriage. Remember: No marriage ever broke up because of too many "I love you's"! Consider saying "I love you" as often as your spouse enjoys hearing it, not just as often as you're comfortable saying it.

Giving Voice to God Awareness

OFFER MEISTER ECKHART'S PRAYER DAILY

If the only prayer you ever prayed was "thank you," that would suffice.

MEISTER ECKHART, 13TH-CENTURY MYSTIC

Gratitude is perhaps the most basic human inclination toward God. We experience what Abraham Joshua Heschel called "the inconceivable surprise of living" and we are spontaneously moved to give thanks. But to whom? Our gratitude is directed to the Gracious Mystery, the Creator, the Life-Giver we call God.

Gratitude is also a basic element in healthy human relationships. Everyone likes to hear the words "thank you." Why not build them into your daily life just as securely as you've built in brushing your teeth before bedtime?

We think that when a lover inflates his loved one he is failing to acknowledge her flaws—"Love is blind." But it may be the other way around. Love allows a person to see the true angelic nature of another person . . .

THOMAS MOORE

A natural place for a daily thank you prayer is at the start or conclusion of a meal. Beginning or ending with a gratitude prayer that emerges from the day's events and from the heart of each person present lends a sense of sacredness to the family meal. Building gratitude into your life and teaching children (if you are parents) about the importance of being thankful can happen in only a few minutes per day.

> ⚷ Begin or end a meal some time soon with each person present simply stating one thing, event, or person for which he or she is grateful. When finished, that person calls on the next person until everyone has had a turn. A daily practice like this can bring gratitude into your home as a permanent resident.

Giving Voice to God Awareness

ASK, "WHERE DID YOU ENCOUNTER GOD TODAY?"

Periodically Claudia and I tell our children to pay specific attention during the day for anything that signifies God's presence. At the end of the day we meet to discuss where God was found. One of our children described this approach to developing spiritual awareness as a "treasure hunt." Each day does indeed hold treasures waiting to be discovered. Talking openly in a family or a marriage about the pearls of learning, joy, wisdom, humor, or just plain fun that we find as we go through our daily lives is a way of voicing an awareness of God, of calling attention to the liturgy of the world.

We are not human beings having a spiritual experience. We are spiritual beings having a human experience.

PIERRE TEILHARD DE CHARDIN

> ⚷ Instead of saying, "How was your day?" when you greet your spouse, try saying, "Where did you encounter God today?" The discussion that ensues will be quite different from the one you're used to having.

RITUALIZING GOD AWARENESS

Just to be is a blessing. Just to live is holy.

ABRAHAM JOSHUA HESCHEL

Everyone has rituals—how she or he makes the morning coffee, reads the paper, or gets ready for bed. In the spiritual realm, a ritual is a habit made holy. It is something we do over and over in a similar manner to evoke an awareness of God. Rituals give us a way of making a commitment to building God awareness into our experience of daily life.

Most people are aware of religious rituals—readings, sacraments, ceremonies—that signal God is present. These are an important part of the liturgy of the Word (church services). When we decide to make marriage a several-decade walk on a sacred path, it is important to create rituals for the liturgy of the world—our daily sphere of living and loving.

We have already discussed one such ritual—building in a gratitude prayer at mealtime. Though this habit is placed in the "giving voice to God awareness" section, it is also a ritual because it can be repeated over and over to create an awareness of the one to Whom we give thanks.

In the *Work on the "I" in Marriage* chapter, we looked at various kinds of habit energies that can get in the way of creating a Namaste marriage. In ritualizing God awareness, we choose to create habits that enhance our daily experience of marriage by keeping us connected to the Ground of our existence.

There are as many potential ways to ritualize God awareness as there are married couples. The sections that follow will present only three. Talk about them and develop your own. Seeing Divinity in disguise and giving voice to our God awareness naturally lead us to wanting to intentionally and regularly create such awareness through simple rituals.

Ritualizing God Awareness

SHARE MEALS AS A SACRED RITE OF THE HOME

In *A Daring Promise*, Richard Gaillardetz points out that the word "companion" comes from the Latin words *com* and *panis,* which together mean "with bread." Sharing food is perhaps the most basic rite of companionship and intimacy with loved ones. It is the ritual that Jesus chose to leave with his closest friends to remember him and make his continuing presence real in their lives after his death. Similarly, the family meal is a ritual in which, by gathering with our loved ones, we remember who we are and invite God's grace to be part of our family experience.

Studies indicate that teenagers from families who eat together regularly are less likely to get into trouble than those from families who rarely eat together. The family meal is a consistent place of gathering in which members of the household can feel a sense of belonging to a supportive and loving group. It sends a regular message to everyone present: "You belong, you are loved."

In our fast-paced culture, it is all too easy for couples or families to fall out of the habit of eating together. If that is the case in your home, consider a family meeting (or more realistically, a series of meetings) to address the issue. Having people commit to being present for a certain number of meals per week and safeguarding that time from other activities is a good way to develop a culture of love and connection in your home.

Many activities, such as children's sports practices, are scheduled during the dinner hour. Rather than allowing such realities to drive the family meal out of your lives, be flexible. It's better to eat together at 8 p.m. than to miss that important family ritual altogether. If there are just too many activities to find a time when everyone can be present, parents can show leadership by discussing the issue of over-commitment with the children in a family meeting and suggesting ways to simplify life. This can be a powerful witness to children about "being a boulder in the torrent of the culture" (see pages 40-42).

All the way to heaven is heaven.

CATHERINE OF SIENA

🔑 Talk with your spouse about how often you want to have meals together as a couple or a family. If entered into deeply, this conversation will lead you to evaluate the variety of commitments that prevent you from sharing meals together as frequently as you might prefer. Include in your visioning meetings a plan to make more regular shared meals a reality.

Ritualizing God Awareness

FRAME THE DAY IN A SACRED WAY

Prayer is our humble answer to the inconceivable surprise of living.

ABRAHAM JOSHUA HESCHEL

Morning and nighttime are the markers of the most primal rhythm of our world. All creatures from the beginning of life on earth have lived in the cycle of light and darkness. Our participation in that cycle can be thought of as a gift, not just a humdrum passing of days. Acknowledging each day as it arrives and reflecting on each day as it ends can be done in surprisingly little time. Beginning a day together with ten minutes of quiet meditation creates a feeling of shared reverence for the gift of life. Ending a day with a brief review of peak or low experiences is a form of prayer. So is simply saying the Lord's Prayer or other brief prayers together. Lighting a candle at the end of the day for a few minutes can be a visual and olfactory reminder of grace. Investing just a few minutes per day in such prayerful rituals can lend a special feeling to your whole experience of marriage and help you recognize God's presence in your home.

Begin your day with a brief bow to one another—hands folded in the prayer position, head tilted forward in an honoring posture. This may sound corny (*Who does such things in this modern world?* you may be thinking), but it is a surprisingly quick and effective way to communicate, "Today will be a day of honoring in our home." As mentioned in the introduction to this book, this "Namaste" greeting literally means "God in me greets God in you." Wow!—is there any marriage that can't use more of that kind of honoring message? If the prior day has been one of conflict or tension, this greeting will serve as a wonderful reset button, but it should not take the place of working through the conflict. (See *Bring honoring to conflict*, practice #3).

Ritualizing God Awareness

CREATE A SHARED VISION FOR INVOLVEMENT IN A SPIRITUAL COMMUNITY

During years of counseling couples, I've asked many people about their spirituality. The most common responses I've received are, "We go to church" or "We really need to get back to church." Sharing and practicing a faith is clearly a central spiritual bond for many couples. In *The Pursuit of Happiness,* psychologist David Myers reviews research indicating that, whereas wealth, gender, race, and education level have little statistical correlation to well-being, active practice of faith is significantly linked to a sense of overall well-being.

In both Catholic and Protestant Christian denominations, about two out of three people in attendance at church on any given Sunday are women. This means that twice as many women go to church as men. It also means that in millions of homes there is tension over the issue of whether to attend church services at all—and if so, how often. Attending church works best in a marriage when there is agreement about the role of religious services in the couple's spiritual life. Failing to clarify this part of the marital vision can lead to ongoing conflict over church services, an aspect of life that is meant to enhance and deepen the quality of marriage, not detract from it.

This aspect of visioning is difficult for many interfaith couples. In such marriages, a shared sense of the liturgy of the world (the sacredness of daily life) may be more readily attainable than an agreement on participating in the same spiritual community. Some couples resolve the problem by having one spouse convert. Others learn to peacefully accept each spouse's choice of faith community. For some couples, the issue of a shared vision in this area causes recurrent conflict. As with all recurrent conflicts (see pages 98-101), it is important to approach the matter with respect and honoring as often as necessary.

Beyond being a place for worship, participation in a faith community provides connection to a human community that encourages reflection on what our lives are about. It allows us to

Survey after survey across North America and Europe reveals that religious people more often than nonreligious people report feeling happy and satisfied with life.

DAVID MYERS

celebrate both our ordinary times and our most significant life events (such as marriages and funerals) in the context of a group of others striving to learn how to live out the ideals of faith, hope, and love. Most churches also provide ample opportunities for allowing daily God awareness to manifest in service to other people within the congregation or beyond.

> ⚷ If your marriage has been one in which church-going causes tension, bring this issue to empathic listening (see pages 87-95). If you are the one more committed to attending church, do not simply try to force your vision on your partner. Listen deeply to one another and see if you can begin to honor each person's unique connection to God and to the spiritual dimension of life. Such mutually honoring energy may help you see the challenge of finding a spiritual community that you are both enthused about in a new way.

SERVING FROM GOD AWARENESS

So far we have explored three aspects of walking the sacred path of marriage: seeing Divinity in disguise, giving voice to God awareness, and ritualizing God awareness. But what good are these if they do not affect how we love others in our home and how we serve in the world? Spiritual awareness is not an end unto itself. It propels us into spiritual behavior, to serve as people helping give birth to the dream of God in the world.

The only ones among you who will be really happy are those who have sought and found how to serve.

ALBERT SCHWEITZER

The ideas in the remainder of this chapter are examples of how awareness of God's nearness in the joys and difficulties of married life can spur us to specific behaviors that contribute to a more loving home and a better world.

Serving From God Awareness

BUILD YOUR MARRIAGE AT THE CROSSROADS

Our marriages have the power to be beacons of hope and love in a world ready to declare the institution of marriage impractical, dead, or at least out of fashion. But to really impact the world, we need to locate our marriages at the crossroads where our private lives intersect with the world.

Think of the hopes and dreams you have for your life together as one road. This book is all about how to travel that road experiencing commitment, intimacy, passion, and spirituality together. To become truly spiritual, however, a marriage needs to exist for something beyond itself. A Namaste marriage cannot consist of attempts to pursue happiness by taking care of only our own needs and desires. Building a new home, taking vacations together, creating a comfortable nest egg for retirement—these are worthwhile pursuits, but if we try to make them all of life, we have not understood the most basic emphasis of Jesus' message: We become truly happy by serving others.

The second road, then, is paved with all of the needs of the world to which committed, loving, passionate people can lend their energies and service.

A marriage which really works is one which works for others. Marriage has both a private face and a public importance.

ROBERT RUNCIE

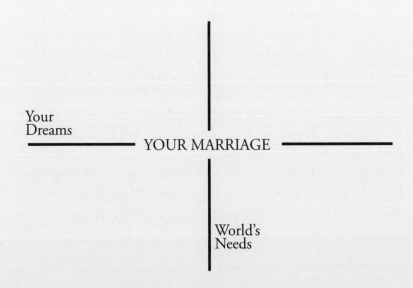

Your
Dreams
————————————— YOUR MARRIAGE ——————

World's
Needs

The purpose of life is a life of purpose.
ROBERT BYRNE

Building your marriage at the crossroads of your dreams and the needs of the world means that service is not just volunteer work that you do occasionally. We're not talking about visiting the crossroads from time to time; we're talking about living there. Service is not an activity we should perform like a chore because we know we're supposed to include it in life. When we live at the crossroads, service to the world grows out of our enthusiasm for life and our desire to give the best of ourselves to the world.

This "build your marriage at the crossroads" idea need not seem too esoteric. If you love gardening, find a way to help others with it. If you have a passion for sports, let it spill over onto children or those who have less opportunity to partake. If you are a skilled business leader, lead others not just to a healthy bottom line but to a deeper sense of what life is about as well.

When people choose work that allows them to serve at the crossroads, their marriages are likely to benefit. Experts on work-family balance refer to positive- and negative-carryover effects from work. Some people come home from work depleted, and their marriages and families suffer for it (negative carryover). People who choose work that is in line with their sense of purpose in life are likely to experience positive carryover. When both work and home are a response to daily God awareness, they support rather than detract from each other.

Just as you and your partner can serve out of your individual God awareness, your marriage also can shine as a ray of hope and service to the world. Reach out to other couples or families. Make hospitality to others a central feature of your home. Consider getting involved in marriage preparation training with your church. If you're raising a family, remind each other regularly how that is a labor of love that places you at the intersection of your joy and the world's great need for strong and loving families. The possibilities for reaching out are endless when we realize that service grows best when it is rooted in what truly energizes our own spirits.

> 🔑 Discuss where your individual passions and your marital relationship intersect with the needs of the world. Talk about whether you live at or only occasionally visit the intersection of personal passion and human needs. How can your daily married life feel more like an extension of your desire to be a positive force in the world?

Serving From God Awareness
HELP HEAL THE WORLD AS YOU HEAL YOURSELVES

You may find yourself thinking, *Finding where my passion intersects with the world's needs sounds good, but I don't know what my passions are.* Some people are inherently more excitable, exuberant, or passionate than others. However, passion is not just about joy. The word also is used to describe the suffering that Jesus endured prior to his death.

Marriage is for better or worse. Every couple gets some of both. Some couples endure difficult ordeals, searing disappointments, or tragic losses together. Couples who begin with grand hopes may find themselves struggling to regain a sense of individual and marital joy after losing a child, working through infidelity, experiencing infertility, or going through other human difficulties. When we serve from our personal experience of the paschal mystery—the mix of suffering and joy that makes up this life—we are capable of bringing a compassion and commitment to service that are not possible if we insist on embracing only the joyful side of life. The crossroads image in the prior section can also symbolize a cross. Service can emerge from what has brought us pain.

As the Dalai Lama wrote in *The Art of Happiness,* everyone on the planet suffers, but it is in railing against this inevitable reality that we create more suffering for ourselves than is necessary. If we stop bemoaning our difficulties, the painful side of "passion"

Here is a simple truth of life that most people never discover. Happy events make life delightful but they do not lead to self-discovery and growth and freedom. That privilege is reserved to the things and persons and situations that cause us pain.

ANTHONY DE MELLO

can give us clues for how to build our lives and our marriages at the crossroads.

When my father was dying, I told my oldest brother Bob that I could not understand why a good man like Dad had to go through such suffering. "I have a feeling his suffering is a gift to us," Bob said. As I lived into the grief of losing Dad, I learned that Bob was right. Suffering cracks our hearts open, and into that raw, exposed place—if we allow it—flows compassion.

Some of the most effective drug and alcohol counselors are those who are themselves recovering from addiction. Married couples who have seen hard times and persevered are powerful witnesses to the potential for forgiveness and healing in programs such as Retrouvaille, which offers hope to distressed couples. If we look, we will find examples all around us of people in the process of healing their own woundedness by reaching out to others suffering the same or similar pain.

The whole story of Jesus' life is about God coming to dwell with us in the glory and painfulness of the human condition. By knowing our experience firsthand, God was able to speak with unquestionable credibility about how a life of love is fashioned. So, too, when we survey both the joyful passion and the painful passion we experience in our lives, we have more than enough material from which to help bring healing to our corner of the Kingdom.

We make a living by what we get, but we make a life by what we give.

NORMAN MACESWAN

You are the light of the world.

JESUS OF NAZARETH

Discuss Henri Nouwen's concept of the "wounded healer"—the idea that those who have known pain are often most effective at being a healing force for others. Discuss at least one way in which each of you is wounded. Talk about how you could turn your pain around in service to the world.

<u>Serving From God Awareness</u>

SEE CREATING A NAMASTE MARRIAGE AS A GIFT TO THE WORLD

There are few things our world needs more than great marriages and families. People learn to love in the context of loving families. Marriage and family together make up the "home school" of love. By investing time and energy into making your marriage the best it can be, you give the world a precious gift. A world made entirely of loving families would have far fewer problems than it has now.

In seeing your marriage and family (if you have children) as gifts to the world, you assign to them their rightful value. If you choose to stay home to raise your children, you are working full-time at something the world sorely needs. If you are balancing working outside the home with creating a loving marriage and family, you too are striving to serve a noble purpose.

Few people on their deathbeds regret not having spent more time at the office. When we begin to think of our marriage and families not as what we create in our leftover time but as our primary life work, we invite a whole new level of potential for these sacred relationships.

The love you give each other can be your greatest service ... If you wish to live lives of service, learn to cherish each other fully. This will not lead to self absorption, but to greater compassion for all.

WILLIAM MARTIN

> In a notebook, write three phrases: "To Each Other," "To Our Children," and "To the World." Under each phrase, list the ways your marriage can be a gift.

To Have and to Laugh

Can She See Divinity in Dis Guy?

Wife: The sacred path in this marriage winds through the kitchen and the laundry before it reaches the bedroom!

Husband: Sure, honey—you mean to pour two glasses of wine and get your negligee out of the dryer, don't you?

Key Summary Points

WALK THE SACRED PATH

- ◆ Each of the other six practices represents a spiritual focus in marriage. Remember that they are not simply techniques for a good marriage—they are forms of spiritual practice to which we return over an over in our efforts to make our marriages the best they can be.
- ◆ Define prayer in a broad sense so that "pray always" makes sense. Think of prayer as any time God breaks through to you or you call out to God. Marriage is full of such moments if you look for them.
- ◆ See Divinity in disguise in your marriage. In particular, learn to see God's presence in whatever brings joy to your spirit. See God, too, in your hard times, helping you cope and leading you to a deeper and more genuine love.
- ◆ Give voice to your awareness of God in married life. In addition to sharing traditional forms of prayer, this may include thinking of "I love you" as a prayer, filling your home with gratitude (Meister Eckhart's prayer), and asking one another how you have encountered God in the day.

◆ Ritualize your God awareness by creating simple, repeatable behaviors that remind you of God's nearness. Examples include sharing frequent meals, beginning or ending the day with prayer, and developing a shared vision for involvement in a faith community.

◆ Let your awareness of God's presence beneath the details of daily life inspire you to loving service at home and in the world. Let your joy and your hardships move you to reach out to serve the world's need. See your extraordinary marriage as a gift to the world.

DISCUSSION QUESTIONS

1. What does it mean to you to say that marriage is a sacred path? Is this a common way of looking at marriage? Have you known couples who consider their married life a sacred path?

2. Do you tend to think of spirituality as mainly involving where you go to church, where you experience God in daily life, or both? Do you think increasing your participation in the liturgy of the world (finding God in daily life) would enhance your experience of the liturgy of the Word (communal worship)?

3. Is your marriage simply a socially approved structure in which you live or is it part of your primary life's work? If it is part of your primary life's work, how much time and energy does your marriage need on a weekly basis to shine brightly to the world?

4. When you think of God's presence in your marriage, do you tend to think of God as a third party who is present primarily at times of formal prayer? Or do you think of God as always present within you and your spouse, your family, and all your daily efforts at loving one another?

NAMASTE

1. *"Hello" or "goodbye."*
2. *"My spirit greets your spirit."*
3. *"God in me greets God in you."*

Acronym for remembering the seven spiritual practices of marriage:

N: Need a shared vision (practice 1).

A: Always stay connected with my spouse (practice 2).

M: Make conflict a path to intimacy by using empathic listening (practice 3).

A: Accept and affirm my spouse "as is" (practice 4).

S: Stay focused on working on the "I" in marriage, not on changing my spouse (practice 5).

T: Treat sex as a sacred gift exchange (practice 6).

E: Extraordinary grace is hidden in the ordinary (spirituality of daily married life, practice 7).

EPILOGUE:
SEVEN PRACTICES, ONE EXTRAORDINARY MARRIAGE

As a way of reviewing and appreciating how the seven practices relate to each other, this section contains a concise overview of the practices—two pages to reload all seven of them in your consciousness when they seem covered over in stress, busyness, or old habit energies.

CREATE A SHARED VISION

Create a shared vision is about making sure you and your partner build your marriage on rock by striving toward shared goals and dreams throughout your marriage. By meeting regularly to discuss your marital vision, you will strengthen your commitment and discover the wonderful things that can happen when you become intentional about turning your individual and marital dreams into realities.

MAKE CONNECTION THE NORM

Creating a Namaste marriage requires a commitment to daily connection. This means that the interaction of the partners is marked by warm greetings, plenty of affection, and words that are respectfully chosen and said in an honoring way. *Make connection the norm* is the spiritual practice of committing to the behaviors that over time make the difference between a close marriage and a distant or troubled one.

BRING HONORING TO CONFLICT

Many couples have great difficulty returning to a close connection after conflict. Their efforts to *Make connection the norm* can be easily derailed by the rub that comes with sharing one's life with another person. *Bring honoring to conflict* means letting your closeness be stronger than your conflict. It means hugging, apologizing, and talking soon after a conflict has subsided instead of distancing, waiting for your partner's apology, or going silent. The "winner" of a marital fight is the first one to offer a hug, apologize, and suggest talking it over in a more honoring way.

Give Up the Search for the Perfect Lover

The experience of falling in love is often based on the illusion that one has found his or her perfect match. This desire for perfect or infinite love is really a longing for God, the Infinite One. By expecting our spouses to be the One who completes us, we do harm to our marriages. Conversely, a Namaste marriage is based on the realization that every human being is finite—and that marriage must be rooted in a deep acceptance of one's own and one's partner's strengths and limitations. Paradoxically, genuine acceptance frees our partner to become his or her best self.

Work on the "I" in Marriage

Coaches are fond of reminding their players that there is no "I" in "team." There is, however, an "I" in marriage, right there near the center of the word. In fact, the word could be spelled "marrIIage" because there are really two "I's" in a marriage. Every married person has some habit energies (patterns of thinking, feeling, or behaving) that help the relationship grow and some that hold it back. All of us have areas in which we can become better individuals and marriage partners. Our marriages go much better when we continue becoming better individuals. Continuing to work on yourself is where you have the most leverage for changing your marriage for the better.

Make Love a Gift

A strong sexual connection is important in marriage because without it married people begin to feel more like roommates, business partners, or friends who are no longer lovers. *Make love a gift* is about focusing one's sexuality on satisfying and delighting one's partner, not on just getting one's own needs met. This approach to sexual loving is inherently other-centered and sacramental. If both of you are focused on giving the gift of your own sexuality in a way that delights your partner, you'll experience the beauty of sexual love throughout your marriage.

Walk the Sacred Path

When we say marriage is sacramental, we don't just mean that it is a sacred ritual that occurs on the wedding day. We mean, rather, that married living and loving continually reveal God's presence in our daily lives. When viewed this way, creating a Namaste marriage can be a primary way that men and women integrate faith and spirituality into their everyday lives. *Walk the sacred path* means seeing Divinity in disguise in your daily life, giving voice to that God awareness, ritualizing it in repeatable behaviors that build up your love, and responding by serving God in your home and in the world.

Diamond in the Middle

This exercise encourages you to consider how the seven practices relate to one another. You will see that they are not seven sequential steps, but rather a set of interrelated practices that support one another.

Create a shared vision is at the center of the seven-diamond image on the cover (or page 14). Here are some questions and thoughts that will help you relate it to each of the other six practices:

- *Make connection the norm:* Is your marriage one in which you have a guiding <u>vision</u> that includes daily closeness (vs. daily stress or distance)?
- *Bring honoring ton conflict:* Do you have a <u>vision</u> for how conflict should be handled? Or do you primarily make it up as you go, perhaps alternating between avoiding conflict and then finding that it comes out in hurtful ways?
- *Give up the search for the perfect lover:* Is your <u>vision</u> for marriage that your partner should meet all of your needs for emotional and physical intimacy? Or does your vision allow that both of you are finite and human—that you will disappoint one another and need to offer acceptance and forgiveness repeatedly throughout your relationship?
- *Work on the "I" in marriage:* Does your <u>vision</u> for marriage take into account that a great relationship requires two individuals committed to continual personal growth? Or do you expect your partner to do most of the growing or changing?
- *Make love a gift:* Do you feel you have a clear and shared <u>vision</u> for your sexual life? Or do you approach it in very different ways that create consistent sexual tension?
- *Walk the sacred path:* Do you have a <u>vision</u> for your spiritual life as a couple? Does it include formal spirituality (prayer or churchgoing), daily spirituality (an awareness of the sacredness of daily life), or both?

You can do the same for each of the seven practices. For instance, if *Walk the sacred path* is placed in the center, reflect on how that practice relates to the others. How does a spiritual sense of marriage affect visioning, staying connected, handling conflict, accepting one another, personal development, and sexuality?

If *Bring honoring to conflict* is placed in the center, a different set of questions arises. How does the way we handle conflict affect our ability to vision together, stay connected, accept one another, work on personal development, have a good sex life, and be spiritually close?

Try placing each of the other practices in the center. What questions emerge? This exercise develops an appreciation that each practice depends on and is linked to the others. Any progress we make on one practice helps us make progress on the others. Likewise, any practice we do not work on will make it harder to practice the others.

GOING BEYOND ORDINARY:
A SAMPLING OF MARRIAGE RESEARCH

Ordinary marriages are normal, which simply means that having an ordinary marriage is the norm. However, this is one aspect of life in which being normal is not the best option. The normal approach to marriage in our culture leads to a divorce rate estimated at somewhere between 50% and 67%.[1] Of couples who remain married, a significant number develop what experts call passive-congenial marriages (the marriage is reduced to a working arrangement that is not a major focus of life) or conflict-habituated marriages (the couple accepts a constant state of conflict and tension as just an inevitable part of being married).[2] Ordinary marriages follow a predictable downward curve in relationship satisfaction. Typically, the drop is steepest after the honeymoon period, levels out after several years, and drops sharply again about seven years into the marriage.[3] Often a steep drop is associated with the arrival of the first baby, with research indicating that positive marital interactions decrease sharply and conflicts increase dramatically when the typical couple makes the transition from twosome to family.[4]

Marriages that are "not too happy" are four times more likely to experience an affair than "very happy" marriages. Furthermore, marriages that are "pretty happy" are twice as likely to experience infidelity than marriages that are "very happy."[5] Apparently, even having a "pretty happy" marriage is not sufficient protection against an affair. While unfaithfulness can never be predicted with 100% accuracy, striving for a "very happy" marriage would appear to decrease the risk of an affair by at least 50%.

Remarkable long-term research begun by Lewis Terman in the 1920's on a group of 1,528 unusually intelligent children has revealed that divorce predicts one's risk of death. Children of divorced parents in the study have had a 33% higher risk of premature death, with those from intact families outliving those from broken families by an average of four years. Researchers who have analyzed cause of death statistics on deceased "Termites" (as members of the group are called) concluded that "parental divorce was the key early social predictor of premature mortality throughout the lifespan." Separated, divorced, or widowed men were found to be at a 120% higher risk of premature death than men who remained in a first marriage. The equivalent risk figure for premature death in separated, divorced, or widowed women was 80%. For men or women currently married but not in a first marriage, the risk of premature death was 40% higher than for those in first marriages.[6]

If the ordinary approach to marriage leads to a high risk of divorce, and divorce predicts earlier death—maybe it's time for a model of marriage that takes us beyond ordinary to extraordinary. Clearly, ordinary marriages are not what couples aspire to when they marry. Their lives are likely to be not only happier and longer if they create extraordinary marriages, but emotionally and spiritually richer as well.

REFERENCES

1   Gottman, J.M. (1993). A theory of marital dissolution and stability. *Journal of Family Psychology, 7,* 57-75.

2   Huston, T.L., Caughlin, J.P. et al. (2001). The connubial crucible: Newlywed years as predictors of marital delight, distress, and divorce. *Journal of Personality and Social Psychology, 80,* 237-252.

3   Kurdek, L.A. (1999). The nature and predictors of the trajectory of change in marital quality for husbands and wives over the first 10 years of marriage. *Developmental Psychology, 35,* 1283-1296.

4   Belsky, J. & Kelly, J. (1994). *The transition to parenthood: How a first child changes a marriage.* (New York: Dell).

5   Atkins, D.C., Jacobson, N.J., & Baucom, D.H. (2001). Understanding infidelity: Correlates in a national random sample. *Journal of Family Psychology, 15,* 735-749.

6   Friedman, H.S., Tucker, J.S. et al. (1995). Psychosocial and behavioral predictors of longevity: The aging and death of the "Termites." *American Psychologist, 50,* 69-78.

FOR FURTHER READING

Couples who wish to learn more about creating a great marriage can benefit from additional reading. Anything by John Gottman, author of the seminal book *The Marriage Clinic* and the world's foremost marriage researcher, is worthwhile. Harville Hendrix's *Getting the Love You Want* can help couples heal recurrent conflicts through awareness of how such difficulties are rooted in childhood wounds. Gary Chapman's *The Five Love Languages,* discussed in Chapter 2 of this book, is a good book for couples to read and discuss together. Judith Wallerstein's work interviewing healthy couples is presented in *The Good Marriage* and is well worth reading. M. Scott Peck's classic book *The Road Less Traveled* presents an insightful definition of love and discusses the disciplines necessary to create long-term loving marriages. Richard Gaillardetz's *A Daring Promise* is a well-articulated spirituality of Christian marriage. William Martin's *The Couple's Tao Te Ching* contains wonderful meditations on love and marriage, especially on the importance of acceptance. Thich Nhat Hanh's book *Anger* is an easy-to-read yet challenging description of the kind of spiritual work that is involved in handling conflict with honoring. Aaron Beck's *Love is Never Enough* can help couples see how negative thinking patterns maximize conflict in marriage and learn to develop healthier thinking habit energies.

KEEP IT CLEAN:
PREVENT TOXINS FROM POISONING YOUR MARRIAGE

Keep it clean is one of the four guidelines given in Chapter 1 for creating a shared vision. If you want to create a Namaste marriage, it is essential that you agree to ban certain problem behaviors or patterns from your marriage. Each of the sections below addresses a problem behavior that, if left unchecked, has great power to damage or destroy your marriage.

ANGER AND DOMESTIC VIOLENCE

Mental health experts are fond of saying that emotions are not good or bad, they just are. This is true about anger. The emotion itself is usually an important indicator of other emotions that hide beneath it, such as hurt, fear, or even love. However, the behavioral manifestations of anger, when not handled appropriately, can do great harm to a marriage.

Appropriate management of anger involves knowing the bodily cues (such as increased breathing or heart rate, heightened muscle tension) that give warning when anger is about to erupt. It also involves knowing the external cues that habitually trigger one's anger and the internal cues (anger thoughts) that throw gasoline on the fire. Learning appropriate ways to communicate about conflict is key (see *Bring honoring to conflict,* practice #3).

If you have an anger problem, go to a local library and search for books on "anger management." Read several books on the topic and try out some of the ideas in your life. If working on your own doesn't help much, get professional assistance. Don't let an excess of anger poison your marriage.

Any intentional grabbing, poking, pushing, slapping, or hitting of a partner is, of course, a major red flag. A single instance of this should lead to setting up marital counseling because allowing it to repeat can lead to a cycle of domestic violence. If there is any sign of a pattern (more than one mild incident), do not pursue marital counseling until the violent spouse completes individual or group treatment for domestic violence. Domestic violence includes more than hands-on harm to one's partner. It includes throwing objects or damaging household items and a pattern of control, intimidation, and contempt.

FOUL LANGUAGE

Using foul language when upset at an object or frustrating situation may not be ideal, but it is not necessarily a serious threat to a marriage. When profanity is aimed at one's partner, however, it constitutes verbal abuse. Allowing a pattern of name-calling to become commonplace in a marriage does not set a loving, sacramental tone for the relationship; in fact, it tears at the very fabric of the marital connection.

If abusive language becomes a problem in your marriage, try banning certain words or phrases by writing them on a list and signing your names to a pledge to rid your marriage of such language. If abusive language persists, go for counseling.

THREATS OF DIVORCE

In group therapy, the most healing therapeutic factor is called cohesiveness. This is the feeling group members get that they are a tight unit capable of supporting one another through whatever difficulties arise for any group member. A marriage is a group of two that also requires an enduring sense of cohesiveness.

There is, therefore, no place for casually threatening divorce in a Namaste marriage. This threat undermines the basis of the marital commitment and the importance of creating a sacramental tone in the marriage. Some people who grew up in homes in which threats of divorce were common may feel that such threats are not a great cause for alarm. They may feel that a threat is just something said "in the heat of the moment." Extraordinary marriages are built on rock-solid commitment. Each threat of divorce replaces some of the rock with sand and eventually results in a foreboding sense that the marriage can be washed away in a storm.

If divorce becomes a serious consideration for one or both partners, it is best dealt with by going for counseling, not by issuing threats. Similarly, frequent threats of breaking up during the dating or engagement period should be considered red flags.

CONTEMPT

What Freud called the "id" is that part of the human personality that is focused on getting pleasure for oneself and avoiding pain. It has no regard for others or for societal norms or laws. It is the part that we see come out in young children who say they "hate" their parents when they are upset.

Contempt, the most corrosive of John Gottman's four horsemen of the apocalypse (see pages 133-134), communicates that one's partner is worthless, stupid, or defective. Most mental health experts call it verbal abuse. Contempt is often communicated as much by the tone in which something is said as by the words themselves. Whereas criticism addresses a certain behavior, contempt puts the entire person down. Contempt is extremely harmful to the goal of building up a strong marriage. If contempt becomes a pattern, counseling will likely be necessary to discover its roots and heal the emotional wounds that motivate it and the harm that it has caused.

ALCOHOL OR DRUG ABUSE

All experts agree that drug or alcohol abuse cause major trouble in a marriage. The problem is, however, that one partner often thinks there is a problem while the other denies it. The rule is: If your partner thinks your marriage has a problem because of alcohol or drug use, then there is a problem. Don't waste time arguing about whether there's a problem. The fact that one of you thinks there is means that the marriage has been affected.

Controversy exists among experts in the field of alcohol abuse treatment. Some experts say the research indicates that mild alcohol problems in people who have never shown a pattern of physical addiction can be dealt with by moderating the drinker's intake of alcohol. Other experts believe that abstinence is the only successful approach to treating all alcohol problems. All experts agree that a person who has experienced a severe physical addiction to alcohol needs to embrace abstinence.

If substance abuse is a problem in your marriage, get help. It is not possible to build an extraordinary marriage when substance abuse keeps showing up like a big bad wolf determined to blow it all down.

WORKAHOLISM

Many marriages suffer from the fact that one or both spouses are more committed to their work than to the marriage or family. In *The Time Bind,* sociologist Arlie Hochschild reports research she did on employees of a large midwestern corporation. She found that many considered work to be a haven from the pressures and stresses of home life. For some people, according to Hochschild, "there's no place like home" has been replaced by "there's no place like work."

Often workaholics justify their long hours because the family needs the money. In many cases, however, the couple is caught in a cycle of spending that forces them to keep working longer hours. Juliet Schor, author of *The Overworked American* and *The Overspent American,* used the image of a squirrel trying to run in a spinning circular cage to capture the feeling that many people have of working harder and harder, only to spend more and more, which then requires more work. Schor calls it "getting caught in the squirrel cage of work and spend."

Some workaholics fail to see the pattern because they say they absolutely love their work. The fact that you love your work does not inoculate your marriage or family against the dangers of workaholism. In fact, loving one's work too much can make it like a drug which one relies on for feeling good.

Recent research indicates that children of workaholic fathers suffer many of the same problems as children of alcoholics. These problems include increased anxiety, depression, and externalized locus of control (feeling controlled by outside factors rather than in control of one's life).

Confronting workaholism can involve dealing with issues of self-esteem, definitions of success, fears about money and security, or a need to live up to a parent or other figure. Counseling may be necessary to untangle the issues that drive a person or a couple to get caught in the squirrel cage.

LYING

Some people grow up in families in which lying was just the way things were done. You didn't tell Mom or Dad the truth because there would be too much conflict. Often in such families, Mom and Dad lived the cycle of lies that goes with substance abuse, infidelity, or other serious problems. Most often a person lies to his or her spouse to avoid getting in trouble—that is, to avoid conflict. However, lying undermines the trust that is the foundation of a strong marriage.

Overcoming the tendency to lie involves learning to handle conflict directly and calmly. When a couple believes in their ability to process conflict, lying withers like a weed pulled up by its roots. See practice #3 (*Bring honoring to conflict*) to learn about how to deal effectively with conflict.

JEALOUSY AND POSSESSIVENESS

When she was young, our oldest daughter took an interest in developing a butterfly collection. As beautiful as those creatures are, collecting them by euthanizing them with poison and pinning them to a display board left me a little conflicted about the new hobby.

This is what some married people do to their spouses. They are so jealous that someone else might become involved with their spouse that they begin to kill off their partner's spirit, to pin her or him to a life of constant, "Where are you going?" or, "Where were you?" queries. This pattern sometimes leads to false accusations of infidelity.

The most common issue underlying possessiveness and jealously is low self-esteem. A jealous person thinks, "I'm not good enough—someone better will take my spouse away from me." Counseling is often necessary to address this pattern because it is usually rooted in a lifetime of poor self-concept, often coupled with having seen infidelity as a way of life in one or more parental figures.

Jealous and possessive spouses need to learn to "let the butterfly go." This means confronting fear and insecurity by deliberately allowing your spouse more freedom than you are comfortable with. This may be extremely difficult for some people who have felt "burned" in past relationships. Counseling can help people realize that working on oneself can lead to personal growth and a reduction of jealousy, whereas attempting to control one's spouse only poisons the relationship.

Over-Reliance on Family of Origin

A few years ago, while walking along a scenic creek near our home, I saw a sycamore tree leaning way out over the water. The tree was more horizontal than vertical, and I expected that it would die soon after its roots pulled out of the bank of the creek. The tree, however, appeared to have a different plan. A surprisingly large secondary tree was growing vertically out of the base of the main tree. A few months later, I returned and found the largest part of the sycamore lying in the creek. It had broken off just above where the secondary tree emerged from its trunk. The root system, relieved of the tremendous leverage of the leaning main tree, remained intact and will continue to serve the offshoot tree for many years to come.

Married partners need to be careful to prevent the weight or influence of their original families from taking down the new tree that is their marriage. We cannot (nor in most cases would we want to) get rid of our family roots, but we need to let them serve the new tree of marriage. This involves some degree of letting the old tree go.

Some people allow their parents or other family members to have more influence on important marital decisions than their spouses. The first few years of marriage often involve an adjustment to making the marriage relationship primary. Each marriage partner may still rely heavily on the family system in which he or she was raised.

Allowing one's parents more power in a marriage than one's spouse is a sure way to poison your attempt to build a Namaste marriage. Family of origin issues are often recurrent conflicts (see pages 98-101) that require ongoing communication. The best prevention for this marital toxin is to engage in your own marital visioning process through regular meetings, making sure that you are creating a relationship with its own future determined by the two of you, not by your parents or in-laws. If these issues become too problematic, consider counseling.

Pressured Sex

Sex should be a given in marriage, by which I mean that 1) it is fundamental to the marriage bond, and 2) it should never be a "taken."

Any time non-consensual sex occurs in a marriage, it is a major red flag. Immediate professional help should be sought. The issue becomes less clear if we consider the more common problem of sexual pressure. The spouse who wants sex more sometimes uses considerable overt or nonverbal pressure to try to get his or her partner to consent. This pattern does not allow for the emergence of a healthy gift exchange approach to sexuality (see practice #6, *Make love a gift*).

The entire sixth chapter of this book presents practices for creating a sacred sexuality in your marriage that will have no place for sexual pressuring.

SEXUAL ADDICTION OR AVERSION

If one spouse develops an aversion to sexuality (perhaps because of hurts in the marriage, past sexual abuse, performance anxiety, health problems, or other factors) the marriage is likely to become troubled. Sometimes the aversion signals a significant lack of emotional connection or the presence of marital toxins such as chronic anger or abusive interactions that eliminate nearly all sexual desire. When sexuality is consistently avoided in marriage, the relationship begins to feel at best like "brother and sister," and both partners know that something important is missing.

Conversely, an addiction to sexuality—as evidenced by constant pressure to have sex, use of pornography, or extramarital relationships—can cause great harm to a marriage.

I sometimes tell my clients that human sexuality is like a chainsaw. If one knows how to use it well, it can be a marvelous tool, even one capable of sculpting beautiful carvings. However, the same tool has the power to be very destructive. It can injure you in a second if you don't use it with care. The analogy breaks down, however, when we realize that a chainsaw cannot hurt anyone if it is not used at all, but the same cannot be said of sexuality in marriage.

Healthy sexuality lies in the golden mean between aversion and addiction. If finding a healthy mean is difficult in your sexual relationship and doesn't seem to improve with your own efforts, get professional help. Don't spend a lifetime together allowing sex, a part of marriage that has such potential to build up your love, to tear it down instead.

SLEEPING APART

Sleep together. This may sound like stating the obvious. *Of course married people should sleep together,* you may be thinking. Some married couples, however, feel it is acceptable to sleep separately if there has been an argument. Sometimes this occurs infrequently at first, and then after a while, the couple sleeps separately most of the time. Sleeping separately should not be used to deal with conflict. Sleeping together, even during hard times, is a powerful symbol of the commitment that is at the foundation of your marriage.

Often couples say that sleeping separately began as a way to deal with snoring or some other problem that made sleeping peaceably in the same bed difficult. My clinical experience, however, indicates that even if that is how it began, sleeping separately usually leads to greater emotional and physical distance between spouses. If the reason for sleeping separately truly is only a practical problem that cannot be resolved (for instance, "He thrashes so much all night long that I can't sleep"), it is important for couples to create connection rituals, such as snuggling in bed before one or both retire separately for the night, to maintain emotional and physical intimacy.

INFIDELITY

It hardly needs to be stated that infidelity—sexual or emotional—seriously damages the marriage bond. Couples can recover from infidelity, but the process is usually long and difficult. It is, quite simply, impossible to build a Namaste marriage when the basic foundation of faithfulness to the relationship is being violated. Having an affair means deceiving one's spouse, leading a double life, and sacrificing one's integrity.

The best approach to affairs, of course, is prevention. Just as childproofing a house cannot provide a guarantee against breakage, there is no fail-safe way to ensure that an affair will not occur in your marriage—at least as long as human beings remain free to make good and bad choices. Being actively involved in building an extraordinary marriage—including the abilities to process conflict and create a mutually satisfying emotional and sexual intimacy—is the best way to affair-guard your marriage.

Many couples turn to counseling when an affair is revealed. Even if the affair occurred some time ago and its effects have lingered, counseling can help.

CHILD ABUSE

Many parents today struggle with finding the balance between gentleness and firmness. Teaching children to honor their parents is as important now as it was when Moses came down from the mountain with the commandment, "Honor you father and your mother." However, teaching parents to honor the rights of their children to grow up in a loving environment is also a matter of great spiritual and societal importance.

Any physical, emotional, or sexual abuse of children is clearly extremely damaging to a marriage and family. If you come from a family in which any of these occurred, it is best to address such issues in counseling before you have children. Once physical or sexual abuse happens in your family, legal authorities may step in. Keeping the family together and making it healthy again after this happens are at best a major challenge.

Emotional abuse is harder to define. Child protection agencies rarely remove an emotionally abusive parent from the home. However, the damage created by emotional abuse (a consistent pattern of degrading or tearing down a child's sense of self) can be crippling. If emotional abuse has occurred in your family of origin or your marriage, I strongly recommend that you seek professional help. Left unchallenged and unaltered, the scars created by an enduring pattern of such abuse may be extremely difficult to heal.

TRIANGULATION

An unusually quick way for a counselor to assess how family members feel about their life together is to ask each person to arrange the family in the room like a living sculpture. As each person takes a turn, a visual image of the family dynamics appears in how the living sculpture is created. I also ask each family member to physically arrange the family in my office to symbolize how they would like the family to function. Almost every family with whom I've done this exercise has chosen the image of a circle to represent the ideal model for their life together. Great families are indeed circles of love.

Triangulation, on the other hand, is a fancy word therapists use to talk about a child becoming caught in a dysfunctional communication pattern between parents. The most common pattern occurs when one spouse begins to share confidences with a child that are not shared with the marriage partner. This sets up an unhealthy dynamic that can create significant problems in the marriage or family. Usually triangulation occurs when a marriage is already burdened by conflict that is not being addressed in a straightforward manner. Using the seven-step model of conflict resolution (see page 77) will make triangulation unlikely and unnecessary in your marriage.

REFUSAL TO GO FOR COUNSELING

What would happen if you owned an automobile jointly with another person but didn't agree on what to do when it broke down? Suppose you wanted to pay a mechanic to fix it, and the other owner believed in just patching it up with "a lick and a prayer" without spending money on professionals. Or suppose the car ran, but the steering wheel was vibrating badly, and you wanted it fixed and your co-owner didn't. That could cause some tension and expose you to considerable risk.

This is exactly how many married couples behave when their marriage needs a professional tune-up. One partner suggests it and the other says, "I don't think there's a problem" or, "Sure, we have a little problem, but we don't need anyone else's help." Often the response is, "It's not our problem, it's *your* problem. *You* go see a counselor if you want to, but *I'm* not going." Marriage counselors often feel like mechanics who are asked to help fix a burned up engine after the owners neglected to change the oil for five, ten, twenty years or more. Thinking that going for counseling is a sign of weakness, people usually wait too long to get professional help for their marriages.

There's a simple way to avoid this unfortunate kind of conflict about whether or not to go for marriage counseling. I call it the "no questions asked" rule. Simply put, this rule means that if one partner asks to go for marriage counseling, the other partner agrees to go "no questions asked" (without trying to talk the partner out of it) and to remain committed to attending counseling to help improve the marriage. This may require going to several counselors before finding the professional who can offer the kind of help you need and with whom both spouses are comfortable. Going to one session and saying, "That was a waste of time—I told you those people are quacks!" does not live up to the commitment required by the "no questions asked" rule.

Some people may avoid a counselor because they do not "believe" in counseling or feel everything should be worked out in the privacy of one's home. Some may have had a not-so-good past experience with a counselor. The key elements of finding a good counselor are getting good recommendations from people you trust and being willing to try several, if necessary, to find a good fit.

Research reviewing results of thousands of studies of counseling or therapy has revealed that four common factors are most responsible for determining if counseling will be helpful. The most important factor is the client. If you go to counseling as an individual or a couple, your own genuine desire to learn and change is the largest determinant of whether the counseling will be helpful. No coach can do much for someone who is not coachable or who does not want to learn.

The second most important factor is the therapeutic relationship that you form with the counselor. This is another term for chemistry or the feeling of fit between you and the counselor. It's unlikely you will gain much from counseling if you don't like the counselor or aren't willing to try out what she or he suggests. If you go to counseling as a couple, both spouses need to feel a good chemistry with the professional. Be sure to choose someone who is able to convey hope (the third most important common factor) and who uses techniques that seem suited to your problems (fourth factor).

Be humble enough to get outside help when it's needed. Going to marriage counseling can be a part of your extraordinary marriage journey, not a judgment against it. People in Namaste marriages are willing to do whatever it takes, and that may include counseling.

EMPATHIC LISTENING: AN EXTENDED EXAMPLE AND FURTHER CONSIDERATIONS

Paul and Joanna have been married for nineteen years. Here is a portion of an empathic listening session between them. Empathic listening skills are indicated in brackets.

Joanna: Is it OK if I go first? [**Determining speaker and listener roles**]

Paul: Sure. I'll do my best to listen.

Joanna: It seems to me that money has been causing a great deal of tension between us lately. I felt very hurt when you were so upset about the credit card bill the other day. It felt like I was being criticized for spending too much, when I've actually really been trying to shop wisely. [**Using "I language"**]

Paul: So that outburst I had really stayed with you and has been bothering you, especially because you felt I was questioning your choices about money—is that what you're saying? [**Reflection**]

Joanna: Yes, when that happens I feel like this little girl who's in trouble or something, and I don't like that feeling at all. Like I've committed a crime or a sin by just buying clothes for the kids.

Paul: Sounds like my angry tone of voice really gets to you. Do you feel I'm more like an angry father than a husband at that point? [**Reflection followed by an opening up question**]

Joanna: Yeah, my dad got angry a lot over little things. When you get so angry, I flip into this mode from the past. I want us to find some other way to deal with money.

Paul: Your dad's anger was difficult for you . . . [**Reflection**]

Joanna: Yeah, I know you're not him, but I feel that way when you get really angry. It just makes me tense up big time.

Paul: What's the tensing up like? [**Opening up question**]

Joanna: Oh, I don't know, just like at that moment I'm not your equal or something, like I have to justify my actions. Each time you do the bills, I can feel this knot inside. I'm just waiting for the same question: "What's THIS expense for?"

Paul: So this tensing up sounds like it really affects our relationship? Is that right? [**Reflection and opening up question**]

Joanna: It's not like I try to hold onto it, but it definitely makes me more guarded on a day-to-day basis. Sometimes I feel like I have to hide things or not talk about the day if I've spent money, even on just groceries.

Paul: So it does affect you more than just when I'm doing bills. Is that what you're saying? [**Reflection**]

Joanna: Yeah, I'd say so. Anyway, thanks for listening. Can I hear how it feels from your side? [**REQUEST TO SWITCH ROLES**]

Paul: Well, I just feel really uptight about the whole college tuition mountain and retirement—how are we going to handle these things when we seem to be able to save so little? Then I get frustrated at my own earning power. Why do teachers make twenty percent of what lawyers make? It gets frustrating. [**"I" language**]

Joanna: So you're saying that you see a lot of big expenses coming up and you're worrying about how we'll deal with them. And you're frustrated that what you really enjoy doing isn't rewarded as well as a lot of other things. Is that close? [**Reflection**]

Paul: Yeah, it sounds crazy, but sometimes these bills are almost like attacks on my masculinity. Shouldn't I be earning enough that I don't have to worry about every little purchase? Is it "successful" to do what you want but struggle along with a modest income?

Joanna: So you're feeling a lot of pressure to provide and maybe like you should be more of a success, whatever that is—is that it? [**Reflection**]

Paul: Yeah, I guess money has the ability to trigger some strong stuff in both of us. I'd like for us to handle that better somehow. Thanks for listening.

Notice how both Paul and Joanna listened, in part, by using reflections. These are nothing more than telling your partner in your own words what you have heard him or her say. Notice also how the reflections ended with a question to convey that the listener wanted to make sure that he or she understood the other person clearly. Ending with a question conveys that you recognize that only your partner can tell you whether you have truly heard his or her feelings.

Notice how neither denied the other's feelings, said they were wrong, or switched to talking about her or his own feelings. Each simply reflected what was said in his or her own words. This looks easy on paper, but it is difficult. When you first try it on a challenging issue in your relationship, it feels like you're trying to talk on one phone to your spouse while listening on another phone to your own mind telling you that you need to convince your partner that he or she has it all wrong. The key is to simply put the phone call from your own mind on hold. Once you get that trick, empathic listening can begin to happen.

One skill that can help us learn to listen deeply is what I call the "Columbo" approach. If you never saw the Columbo whodunit program on television, he was a detective who played dumb to get the bad guys to incriminate themselves. His approach was to appear like a bumbler, but he was, in fact, sly as a fox. What does Columbo have to do with empathic listening? Often we fail to listen deeply to our partners because in our own minds we say, "I've heard all this before; there's nothing new here." In effect, we think we've already solved the case before our partner has his or her say. Once we say or think, "I know, I know—I've heard it all before," listening stops. We might even think that we not only know everything our spouse is going to say about this issue, but that we know our spouses so well they can say nothing that will be new to us on any topic. This attitude is unfortunate and blocks efforts at discovering new insights about our partners.

The Columbo approach involves suspending the belief that you know your partner completely and treating each statement like it's the first time you've heard it. In doing this, we might actually sound a bit like Columbo:

> *"Now I'm not sure—I could have this all messed up. Let me see if I'm getting it. Are you saying that it hurts you when I leave my socks and underwear on the floor because it makes you feel like a maid? Is that what you're saying, or have I totally missed it?"*

This is how Columbo talked to his prime suspects—acting like he could barely understand what was unfolding. The example above might be a bit exaggerated for how we should talk to our spouses during empathic listening. Nonetheless, the basic idea is to presume that you don't have the mystery solved, that there's something new to be learned from your spouse by listening deeply.

Remember, empathic listening will rarely, if ever, happen *during* a conflict. It is a skill to be used to heal the tension after a conflict or to be used to share positive heart-to-heart emotions whenever you choose.

RESISTANCE TO CREATING AN
EXTRAORDINARY, NAMASTE MARRIAGE

When a worthwhile goal requires work and sustained commitment, human beings often find myriad reasons to convince themselves that the goal is really not so worthwhile after all. Sometimes we actively resist what we know is in our best interests because we don't believe in our ability to achieve the goal. Imagine asking a couple on their honeymoon the following questions:

- Would you like to have a committed marriage that lasts a lifetime?
- Would you like to continue to share fun, laughter, affection, and heart-to-heart conversations with your mate?
- Would you like to be passionate lovers throughout your entire marriage?
- Would you like to be spiritual partners as well, helping one another grow closer to your full human potential and to God?

Few newly married couples would answer these questions in any way other than, "Yes, yes, yes, and yes!"

By the time many people are several years into marriage, however, they've begun to lose the dream. They are like grown-ups who have lost the unbridled enthusiasm of young children. They convince themselves that life is busy and that they just need to accept things the way they are, which is often rather, well, ordinary.

What are some of the specific ways a person might resist creating an extraordinary, Namaste marriage? We will explore four below.

"DON'T ROCK THE BOAT"

Perhaps the most common resistance goes something like, "We've always done it this way, and I see no need to rock the boat."

How long would you stay in the room if your doctor said, "I've always practiced medicine the same way and I don't believe in any of the technology that's been invented since I was in medical school in the 1970's"? What if your accountant said she doesn't believe in keeping updated on changes in the tax code because "I always do tax returns the same way anyway"?

Or how about if a painter said, "All that concern about lead in the paint is a lot of nonsense—I've been using lead-based paint for my whole career."

An unprofessional attitude is easy to spot in these examples, but we don't sound much different when we say, "We've always done it this way" about our marriages.

"I'M NOT INTO TOUCHY-FEELY"

Some of us might encounter resistance in our minds like, "I'm not into all this touchy-feely stuff."

Can you imagine a baseball player telling his coach, "I'm not into fielding" or a football player saying, "I'm not into physical contact"?

Affection, romance, expressing love, talking heart-to-heart, sharing prayer and spirituality—all these and more are integral parts of married life "played" at the highest level. If we try to cut them out we could find ourselves sitting on the sidelines wondering why we're not in the game of creating a great marriage.

In marriage workshops, I stress to both men and women that an enjoyable, loving, spiritual sex life flows from the heart-to-heart connection of the couple. That usually gets the attention of some of those who are prone to thinking that they can just skip all the "soft" stuff.

Keep an open mind. Be willing to go back to basics and learn something new. If even one idea from this book helps you create a better marriage, reading it will be worth your time.

"WHO HAS THE TIME?"

Another common resistance to building a Namaste marriage is, "It sounds great, but who has the time?" Most of us believe that our time is not our own. We don't realize that the way we spend our time is an ongoing statement about what we value most in life. Saying "I don't have time for an extraordinary marriage" is the same as saying "I don't value my marriage enough to make it extraordinary."

The illusion that there is no time is very difficult for many people to overcome. They believe that life is just inherently busy and that there's very little time left for a higher quality marriage. This illusion is perpetuated because nearly everyone we meet agrees with us that life is so hectic it leaves us falling in bed night after night exhausted so we can get up and do it all again tomorrow.

Building a Namaste marriage requires us to be countercultural. We need to be clear about what the most important things are in life and allocate our time and energy so that we keep first things first.

"WE COULD NEVER HAVE AN EXTRAORDINARY MARRIAGE"

Still others may be resigned to living with an ordinary or troubled marriage because they believe their relationship contains serious irreconcilable problems. The best that can be done, these people think, is just to live with the problems and give up on hoping for the marriage that they really want. These people seem to prefer the empty feeling of avoiding problems to what they imagine will be the pain stirred up by trying to make the marriage better. Because their problems seem to be unfixable, one or both spouses give up on actively working to improve the marriage.

Extraordinary marriages have unfixable problems too, but the couple establishes an honoring process for engaging these problems as they surface repeatedly in the relationship. Most marital problems become entrenched because the couple is at a loss for what to do about them. They feel that rebuilding a warm, loving, passionate marriage would be like trying to build a fire without matches or even two sticks to rub together. They don't think they have the tools to get the job done, and they may even believe the tools simply don't exist. The seven-practices model contains the needed tools!

There are undoubtedly more than four ways to resist making your marriage all it can be. It's OK to have resistance. Most of us resist change in anything that is familiar to us, even if what is familiar is not very satisfactory. Growing as an individual and in marriage, however, requires us to step beyond our resistance into the world of openness to ongoing learning.

ACKNOWLEDGMENTS

First and foremost, I express my gratitude to Claudia, with whom I have had the privilege of living and refining the seven practices. This book is an expression of both my professional training and my lived experience of marriage with a woman deeply committed to continued learning and growth. Her review of earlier drafts of this book were helpful, but more important, her willingness to attempt to live with me what I have written about has been indispensable to the development of the seven-practices model.

I am grateful to Lucy Abu-Absi and Reverend Daniel Zak for their support of my marriage training work in the Catholic Diocese of Toledo, Ohio and their willingness to read and comment on early drafts of this book. Judy Ludwig also read early drafts and contributed her editing expertise.

To all the couples who have attended my marriage training over the years, and to the thousands of married couples I've had the privilege of knowing as a psychologist, I express my thanks. I admire your courage and your willingness to continue trying to learn more to make your marriages the best they can be.

ABOUT THE ARTWORK

Artist Phil Harris created the symbolic portrayal of the seven practices on the cover and on the first page of each chapter. They were created on ceramic tiles, each fired at high temperature. The symbolism contained in the individual tiles is discussed on the first page of each chapter. Symbolic elements that pertain to the seven-diamond image as a whole include:

◆ The pyramid in the center tile, representing the couple's shared vision, appears to have been dropped like a rock in the center of a pond. Its effects ripple out to the other six practices.

◆ The wavy "energy" lines appearing to flow from the cracked vessel in the bottom diamond emanate upward through the piece to the top diamond. Symbolically this conveys how acceptance and giving up the search for the perfect lover (bottom tile) leads to the experience of daily married life as sacred (top tile).

◆ Two large diamonds (each made of four smaller diamonds) overlap on the small center diamond (which represents creating a shared vision). This depicts how two individuals form a marriage by interconnecting their lives and creating a dynamic vision for their relationship.

Phil Harris can be contacted at: PO Box 275, West Park, NY 12493   (845) 384-6396   claycouple@msn.com

PERMISSIONS

Quotations from *The Couple's Tao Te Ching* by William Martin, © 2000 by William Martin, used by permission of the publisher, Marlowe and Company, a division of Avalon publishing group.

Quotations from *The Road Less Traveled: A New Psychology of Love, Traditional Values, and Spiritual Growth,* © 1988 by M. Scott Peck used by permission of the publisher, Touchstone, a division of Simon & Schuster.

Quotations from *The Good Marriage: How and Why Love Lasts,* © 1996 by Judith Wallerstein and Sandra Blakeslee used by permission of the publisher, Warner Books, a division of Time Warner Book Group.

List of perpetual issues from *The Marriage Clinic* by John Gottman, © 1999 by John Gottman, used by permission of the publisher, W.W. Norton and Company.

Order Form for CLB Press

The Seven Spiritual Practices of Marriage: Your Guide to Creating a Deep and Lasting Love
ISBN: 0972835505 224 pages, paperback, $16.95

Quantity: _____

      X <u>$16.95 ea.</u>

TOTAL 1: _____

Divinity in Disguise: Nested Meditations to Delight the Mind and Awaken the Soul
Selected one of the best spiritual books of 2003 by *Spirituality and Health* magazine.
ISBN: 0972835504, 192 pages, hardcover, $19.95

Quantity: _____

      X <u>$19.95 ea.</u>

TOTAL 2: _____

Shipping and Handling: Add $2.95 for first book ordered and $1.95 for each additional book.

S & H: _____

SUBTOTAL: _____ (Add Total 1, Total 2, S & H)

Tax: Add 7.25% sales tax to Subtotal if you live in Ohio
or provide tax exempt number: _____

TAX: _____

ORDER TOTAL: _____ (Subtotal + Tax)

Make check payable to CLB Press and mail to: CLB Press, PO Box 74, Monclova, OH 43542.

YOUR SHIPPING INFORMATION:
Name: _____
Address: _____
City/State: _____ ZIP _____
Allow three weeks for delivery

Note: For orders of quantities of ten or more books, please contact us at <u>CLBPress@buckeye-access.com</u>,
call (419) 861-2269, or write to CLB Press, PO Box 74, Monclova, OH 43542